Narrowing the Nation's Power

W9-AVT-300

Narrowing the Nation's Power

The Supreme Court Sides with the States

John T. Noonan, Jr.

UNIVERSITY OF CALIFORNIA PRESS

Berkeley   Los Angeles   London

University of California Press
Berkeley and Los Angeles, California

University of California Press, Ltd.
London, England

First paperback printing 2003
© 2002 by the Regents of the University of California

Library of Congress Cataloging-in-Publication Data

Noonan, John Thomas, 1926–.
    Narrowing the nation's power : the Supreme Court sides
with the states / John T. Noonan, Jr.
        p.   cm.
    Includes bibliographical references and index.
    ISBN 0-520-24068-5 (pbk : alk. paper)
        1. Governmental liability—United States—States.
2. State governments—United States—Privileges and
immunities.   3. United States. Supreme Court.   I. Title.

KF1322.N66   2002
342.73'088—dc21   2002019473

Manufactured in the United States of America
11   10   09   08   07   06   05   04   03
10   9   8   7   6   5   4   3   2   1

The paper used in this publication meets the minimum
requirements of ANSI/NISO Z39.48-1992 (R 1997)
(*Permanence of Paper*). ∞

There are some things which the General Government has clearly a right to do—there are others which it has clearly no right to meddle with, and there is a good deal of middle ground, about which honest & well disposed men may differ. The most that can be said is that some of this middle ground may have been occupied by the National Legislature; and this surely is no evidence of a disposition to get rid of the limitations in the constitution; nor can it be viewed in that light by men of candor.

Alexander Hamilton to George Washington,
August 18, 1792

CONTENTS

ACKNOWLEDGMENTS

I am indebted to the help of Ailsa Chang, Claire Ebey, Raymond C. Fisher, William Hapiuk, Christopher Hazuka, Cassandra Joseph, David McGowan, Jeffrey McKenna, John K. Noonan, Rebecca Lee Noonan, Philip Rohlik, Elizabeth Storz, Quyen Ta, Jeffrey Wu, and Julie Zampa.

I appreciate particularly the secretarial skills of Evelyn Lew.

Berkeley, California
December 8, 2001

PROLOGUE: A RECURRENT STRUGGLE IS RESUMED

If you were a writer whose short stories were published by an ethnic press affiliated with the University of New Mexico, you would be justifiably surprised to learn that, when your publisher disregarded your copyright, you could not sue for damages because the press was a sovereign entitled to a sovereign's immunity from suit. If you were a professor of business at the University of Montevallo in Shelby County, Alabama, and were passed over for a raise because of your age, you would be understandably indignant to learn that your university, classified as a sovereign, could not be brought to court for violating federal law against discrimination based on age. If you were a woman attending a state college and you were raped by several members of the football team, you would be more than outraged to discover that, when state authorities did nothing to punish the rapists, federal law was helpless to make up for their deficiency. Yet these and similar results have been reached in the last five years because of judgments of the Supreme Court of the United States.

The results are incomprehensible without an understanding of the legal doctrines on which they are based. The doctrines are abstract. Abstractness gives them an appearance of depth they do not deserve. They do, however, have to be put in the context provided by the constitution of the United States, which governs one nation and fifty states. It is as the protector of the fifty states that the Supreme Court has developed the doctrines that were decisive in these cases.

"[T]he States entered the federal system with their sovereignty intact." If written in 1791, this sentence would have been understood as an anti-federalist's reservation as to the constitution. Uttered fifty years later in 1841, it would have expressed the new sectionalism and, in particular, the sensitivity of the South to any Northern encroachment on its peculiar institution of chattel slavery. But this statement was not made in 1791 or 1841. It was made in 1991 and was not made by an anti-federalist or a potential secessionist. It was made by the Supreme Court of the United States.

The Supreme Court repeated this statement with approbation in 1997 and again with approbation in 1999. It is foundational for the current court's claim that the immunity of sovereigns is enjoyed today by each of the fifty states. To anyone familiar with the precedents of that court or with the text of the constitution of the United States or with the history of the Civil War, it is an extraordinary statement.

In modern jargon, "federalism" is sometimes the caption used to describe the championing of the states at the expense of the nation. It is a confusing misnomer. The old slogan "states' rights" was more accurate in catching the goal of the tendency. Federalism, in its classic use, stands for the recognition of the role of the states in the spheres that the constitution allots them in a framework explicitly conferring great powers on the national government. We are not a confederacy of sovereigns as the secessionists believed. Nor are we subjects of a single unitary government. Our frame of government is more astutely designed. As James Madison, a principal designer of it, expressed the matter, we have "neither a national nor a federal Constitution, but a composition of both." To make "federalism" a slogan for states' rights is to contort the original meaning and to suppress the national component in the original design.

Sovereignty is an ancient concept, and the corollary of sovereignty, to which the statement of the Supreme Court leads, is the immunity of the sovereign from suit, a concept of the common law as old as the monarchy of England. Both concepts—sovereignty and the accompanying immunity—have been given a modern gloss by the Supreme Court that expands them to institutions sponsored by the fifty states. Universities, university presses, university research laboratories, as well as a multitude of other enterprises run by the states, now appear in the robes and dignity of sovereigns. The fifty sovereign states have multiplied into over two thousand entities. The friend of the fifty states, the court has extended to all of them the sovereign's prerogative of freedom from being sued in court for cash.

The ancient and now expanded concepts of sovereignty and sovereign immunity have become of great importance to the Supreme Court and to the country. The concepts have become the court's way of restricting the powers of Congress and enlarging the areas where the states can escape effective control by Congress. Mixed with new criteria created by the court to limit lawmaking by Congress, the sovereign immunity of the states is at the center of an explosive package disturbing the ascendancy of the nation over its parts.

Congress can make laws where the constitution grants it power to make laws. The constitution does that in two principal places. Article I gives Congress authority to legislate on specific subjects, including the coining of money, the making of patents, and the regulating of interstate commerce. These express powers were construed by the Supreme Court under John Marshall to imply other powers, such as the power to create a national bank and to enact any law adapted to the achievement of the express powers.

Under its express powers, Congress can create standards that are as applicable to the fifty states as they are to any individual. The standards apply to the states, but, so the Supreme Court has now determined, they cannot be enforced by a private person getting damages from the states. The standards exist, giving rights to private persons without providing them a monetary remedy. A right without a remedy is a strange animal, as strange in the legal world as a dog with a bark and without a bite in the zoological world. Such is the consequence, the Supreme Court has said, that flows from the sovereignty of the states.

Congress also has power to make laws under the fourteenth amendment. Enacted after the Civil War, the amendment provides that no state shall deprive any person of life, liberty, or property without due process of law or deny to any person the equal protection of the laws. The amendment gives Congress the power to enforce these provisions "by appropriate legislation."

Because the amendment explicitly speaks of the obligation of the states, Congress does have the power, so the Supreme Court has held, to enact legislation subjecting the states to suit. But the Supreme Court has added a qualification restricting even this power. According to the court in 1997, legislation that is appropriate must meet new criteria now set by the court. In the court's words, "There must be congruence and proportionality between the injury to be prevented or remedied [by the legislation] and the means adopted [by the legislation] to that end." "Congruence and proportionality"—these are the criteria Congress must meet. The court determines whether Congress has met them.

Like the statement on the intact sovereignty of the states, this pronouncement was no dictum, no velleity, no ephemeral notion. It was at the heart of an opinion invalidating a law passed almost unanimously by Congress. It has been repeated in subsequent decisions holding void other acts of Congress. It is not a position that will lightly be abandoned. It effects a shift of power from Congress to the federal courts. It makes the federal courts the overseers of what is normally a matter of legislative judgment. As employed by the Supreme Court, the criteria also effect a shift of power from Congress to the states.

The criteria that Congress must meet on pain of the voiding of its legislation work in tandem with another new criterion also announced in 1997 by the Supreme Court. Legislation under the fourteenth amendment, the court then declared, must be based on a legislative record sufficient to demonstrate to the court that there is in fact a large wrong or evil that Congress is acting to remedy. Before Congress can lawfully act, it must have before it, the court has stated, a history of "widespread and persisting deprivation of constitutional rights."

This criterion means that the federal judiciary, from the Supreme Court itself down to the federal district court in Guam, may, and indeed must, treat Congress the way courts would treat an administrative agency, whose work will be set aside on appeal if the court finds the record made by the agency not substantial enough to justify the agency's rulings. Rigorous in itself, this criterion has been made more rigorous by the Supreme Court's dismissal of what it has styled "anecdotal evidence," with the implication that stories testified to by witnesses before congressional committees are not enough to justify legislation. In this way an act of Congress is subjected to stringent judicial scrutiny to determine the nationwide extent of the evil against which the act is directed. In contrast, the Supreme Court's own announcement of constitutional law, binding on the whole country, is based on the record compiled in a single case.

The extraordinary criteria created in 1997 have meshed with the court's doctrine on sovereign immunity to effect what the court sees as the restoration of the autonomy, the dignity, the sovereignty of the fifty states. It is on their behalf that the court has labored. It is on their behalf that it has created the new criteria and extended to the fifty sovereigns it seeks to befriend a significant, although not comprehensive, immunity from suit.

Not as a necessary corollary of these positions but as an understandable offshoot of the mentality and convictions undergirding them, the court has been unwilling to see inaction by the states as a breach of the fourteenth amendment. State action, it knows, is what that amendment governs. In law when there is a duty to act, the failure to perform the duty is action of the gravest kind. Holding unconstitutional the Violence Against Women Act, the Supreme Court has not acknowledged this principle. The quasi-autonomy of the states would have been compromised by its application.

The decisions now to be reviewed have been possible because the constitution has been interpreted by the Supreme Court as confiding to that court the power definitively to interpret the constitution. The power of interpretation functions as the power to revise, restate, remake the constitution, so that the Supreme Court becomes the supreme authority in the land. Robert Jackson, when attorney general of the United States, wrote a book describing the battles, recurrent in our history, of the two elected branches of government with the appointed, life-tenured judiciary that possesses the power to interpret the constitution with finality. He predicted that the battles would resume because the conflicts are inherent in the structure created by the constitution. Jackson entitled his book *The Struggle for Judicial Supremacy*, a title that seemed to imply that it was the story of an effort to attain a desirable end. That implication was denied by the book itself. The court's struggle for supremacy over all branches of government, Jackson argued, had been defeated, would resume, and must be resisted again.

The struggle Jackson foresaw has come again. It has come, in part, because a tension between the nation and the individual states is built into the constitution, and there must be some ebb and flow of power between them. The ancient philosophical tension of the One and the Many takes concrete form in our government. The current court has thrown itself on the side of the many states, seeking to sustain a structural role for them, to bolster their status and to assure a limited autonomy. Because of the overarching federal government, the autonomy must necessarily be limited, the sovereignty of the fifty states must always be a quasi-sovereignty, precariously preserved. Mixing old doctrine and new, the Supreme Court is making a mighty effort to put the states in what the court conceives to be their rightful place.

Newspapers like to predict outcomes of cases in terms of the president who appointed the judges. It's a crude predictive device. Far more important is the life experience of each judge. In most of the cases considered in this book, five appointees of three Republican presidents have outvoted two appointees of a Democratic president and two appointees of two Republican presidents. Presidents and parties will not explain the votes, and I do not intend to enter into a psychobiography of the justices.

I do mention in the text or in endnotes the names of the federal district and circuit judges who participated in the cases. Connoisseurs of the judiciary will appreciate this information, often not provided by the press. And I do identify the members of the Supreme Court majority and the minority in endnotes not stressing the play of personalities.

I focus on the institution rather than the individuals within it precisely because what is happening is an institutional drift, an institutional activity. Individuals, no doubt, play a part. But, as Jackson observed, the institution has more influence on individuals than individuals have on the court. There are divisions in the court. In this area of law, five to four has become the rule. The dissents have had force and eloquence. They are auguries of a better time. Yet sovereign immunity itself is an old judicial invention. It has been expanded without opposition, and, at the time of the court's creation of the new criteria for congressional action, not a single voice on the court was raised in criticism. It is, moreover, not only the individual justices who have a role, but also their law clerks, whose research and writing, especially in the production of histories of constitutional provisions and precedents, underlie the court's opinions. The leadership of the court is also significant. The court cannot take a sharp turn, as it has here, without an agenda and a head. It is better, at least for the purpose of showing the present problems, to look at the court as it functions collectively under its chief.

To emphasize the newness, the unprecedentedness, the surprisingness of certain court decisions in this area is not the same as saying they are wrong. The new departures have been made with great deliberateness, great sincerity, great conviction that they are essential to the preservation of our federal form of government. A number of John Marshall's opinions were also new, unprecedented, and astonishing to many of his contemporaries.

The new constitutional decisions, it is true, do not depend on any words in the constitution. They are boldly innovative. It was once asserted by some members of the present court that decisions were wrong if they were unfaithful to the text of the constitution or lacked fidelity to the original intent of its framers. These criteria are no longer used by these members who form part of the majority of the present court and denounce "ahistorical literalism" in reading a constitutional provision. The court's rejection of "ahistorical literalism" is a turn toward a more adventurous reading of the constitution.

"Activist judge" and its polemical counterpart "strict constructionist" probably should be banished from the political lexicon. The terms should be banished because they cannot distinguish one set of judges from another. The present court is composed of judges often categorized as conservative but in fact highly original in their treatment of the constitution. It is an illusion to suppose that they are less inventive than their predecessors in their interpretation of constitutional texts.

A standard that depends on an illusion is harmful. There are students of politics who maintain that illusions are necessary to preserve the public order or the public's confidence. They say that no institution can be transparent. I reject that unproved contention and reject it all the more vigorously when it is applied to distort discourse about something I'm familiar with. The idea that "activism" is a helpful or accurate or meaningful category for judging the Supreme Court of the United States is an illusion.

Banish the illusion, what are the criteria for judgment? One criterion is logic. A position that is a contradiction in terms is intolerable in any rational discourse. It is my contention, to be developed in the body of this book, that such a contradiction sits at the center of the court's application of the rule of sovereign immunity.

If we could get rid of the illusion fogging debate and the oxymoron masquerading as law, a modest goal would be to set out principle not broken by multiple exceptions. Law without any exceptions is not possible. A principle with many exceptions is barely a principle. Such is the tattered condition of state sovereignty that the current Supreme Court has claimed as a fundamental principle.

Worse still is a principle without a rationale for its existence or a rationale to guide its expanded application. Such is the case of the immunity now accorded the fifty states. No justification for the immunity, so I will argue, has been shown. No limit has been found to its extension to the most ungovernmental of state-promoted activities.

It is my observation in "The Battle of Boerne" that the Supreme Court, in repelling what it saw as an invasion of the judicial domain by Congress, invented criteria for Congress that invaded the legislative domain. It is my contention, developed in dialogic form in the following two chapters, that the Supreme Court, as the devotee of dignity and the hitchhiker of history, has embraced with mistaken enthusiasm a doctrine of state immunity that is overextended, unjustified by history, and unworkable in any consistent way. "The Sovereign Publisher and the Last of the Menu Girls" and "Perhaps Inconsequential Problems" show the unhappy interaction of the new legislative criteria with the doctrine of immunity in the application of the criteria to very old legislation protecting intellectual property and to comparatively new legislation assuring equality to the elderly and the disabled. "Gang Rape at State U." focuses on Congress's effort to provide women with the equal protection of the law, and the Supreme Court's hostile response, in the name of individual liberty and state autonomy, to that effort. "Sovereign Remedy" sets out what I believe should be said and done now in the face of the present danger to the vital balances of our organic national life.

For principle, suppose we turn to the purposes of the people of the United States as the people expressed them in the preamble to the constitution: "to form a more perfect Union, establish Justice, insure domestic Tranquility . . . and secure the Blessings of Liberty."

These grand phrases, it might be thought in a lawyer-like way, are empty, to be filled in by the politics of the day. It is my endeavor here, however, to lay them as criteria alongside the facts of particular cases and to ask if the results of these cases can be squared with the announced purposes of our constitution. Do decisions that return the country to a pre-Civil War under-standing of the nation establish a more perfect union? Are deci-sions just that shield not only the states but lesser appendages of the states from paying for the wrongs they commit? Do deci-sions that leave the elderly and the disabled with inadequate remedies for unequal treatment establish justice? Do decisions that dislodge patents, copyrights, and trademarks from assured protection insure domestic tranquility? Do decisions that deny Congress the power to protect the free exercise of religion se-cure the blessings of liberty? Do decisions that leave women less protected by the law than men achieve any of the constitu-tion's ends?

The rhetorical nature of these questions points to the answers I give. The results I criticize were reached largely, although not wholly, by means of the doctrinal devices—state sovereign im-munity, congruence and proportionality of legislation, and a record of evils to be eradicated—that have no footing in the con-stitution. Remove these obfuscations, it will be clear that the court's decisions do not survive the test of serving constitutional purposes.

In the constitutional balance reached by the court, the fifty states weigh more heavily than the very large numbers poten-tially affected adversely by the court's decisions—for example, the 4.5 million employees of the fifty states and state-related entities; the over 5 million holders of patents; the 10 million holders of trademarks, the 100 million holders of copyright; the over 150 million believers in faiths whose requirements can tran-scend the interest of government; and the one-half of the popu-lation distinguished by gender as women. Only a small fraction of these persons will actually be injured as a consequence of the court's rulings; but small fractions of such large numbers point to the magnitude of the problems the court has created.

This state of affairs invites comparison with other moments in the history of the United States produced by positions taken by the Supreme Court—with *Dred Scott v. Sandford*, holding that Congress could not constitutionally prevent property, including slaves, from being brought into a federal territory; with *Lochner v. New York*, holding that a state could not constitutionally regulate the hours of work of employees of business; and with *Carter v. Carter Coal Company*, holding that Congress could not constitutionally regulate the labor relations of a corporation whose business was coal mining. These decisions all had substantial impact upon the nation. *Dred Scott* helped bring on the Civil War. *Lochner* had a negative effect on the conditions of employment for over a quarter of a century. *Carter* nearly brought the New Deal to an end. Each decision substituted the judgment of judges for that of legislators. Each decision is recognized today as unjustified by the constitution.

The court's effort to give more power to the states has led at the same time to the accretion of power by the court, almost as a promontory's division of the ocean leads to the promontory's accretions from the sea. Accretion is a passive process. It is also actively carried out by agents organic to the accretor. So, too, the court has accreted power from the legislature and the president as it has created various discretions that it may exercise in deciding when immunity exists and when legislation is proportionate and when a legislative record is satisfactory. Active accretion is the work of the institution, not on its own behalf but for the cause of state sovereignty that it has found transcendent.

No one can pretend to know what a perfect balance between the federal government and the fifty states would be, or to know what would be a perfect balance among the three branches of the federal government. Like the biological balances that maintain our lives, these great civic balances are not static, they respond to events, they take shape from experience. Professing ignorance of perfection, I write on the basis of my own experience as a citizen, a person immersed in law for fifty years, and a reader of history to point to what's wrong with the balances now struck. The middle ground has been moved, with unsettling consequences. Our national motto, engraved on our currency and coinage, is *e pluribus unum*—From many, one. It must be not only our motto but our guide.

CHAPTER I

The Battle of Boerne

The big break came with *Boerne.* I tell its story here against the background of the American devotion to religious liberty and the power granted Congress after the Civil War by the fourteenth amendment.

THE LUSTROUS EXPERIMENT

A unique contribution of the United States to civilization is the invention of religious liberty. No nation before our own had moved beyond tolerance. No nation had made freedom of religion a cherished value. No nation had designated "exercise," not mere opinion, as the value guaranteed. No nation had ever guaranteed in a written constitution that the nation would enact no law prohibiting the free exercise of religion.

The mother country, Great Britain, had for a century enjoyed a highly limited tolerance, coupled to the establishment of a church endowed with many prerogatives and privileges. Protestants who were not communicants in the Church of England, Catholics, Jews, members of all the other religions of the world, agnostics, and atheists were the subject of legal disabilities destructive of their civil rights and prohibitive of their participation in the government of the country. Some of the American colonies founded by Englishmen had moved toward greater tolerance, but none before the American Revolution had established equality and complete freedom of religion. All the colonists were part of an empire whose monarch was also the head of a church.

A would-be imitator of America, revolutionary France, adopted a statute guaranteeing freedom of religious opinion shortly before Congress adopted the Bill of Rights, in which the free exercise of religion was set out as our first freedom. The French National Assembly so little grasped the idea of religious liberty that, within months of enacting the statute, the assembly took on the task of reorganizing the Catholic Church in France along the lines of a civil organization. Within two years, freedom of religious opinion in France had disappeared in favor of a sustained, bloody persecution of Catholics and of organized attempts to exterminate Christianity.

The unique United States provision was, therefore, an experiment. It had to be an experiment. It had never been tried before. It was proclaimed as an experiment by its principal proponent, James Madison, who also drew the corollary that the umpire of the experiment would be experience. It has been the American experience that has determined the success of the experiment and its extent and contours.

The experiment at first was modest. The guarantee bound only the fledgling nation. It did not bind the thirteen states. A number of them, especially in New England and the South, had established churches. The states had no intention of giving them up. New Hampshire even had a provision that only Protestants could be elected to the state senate, and as this body elected that state's United States senators, New Hampshire indirectly violated article VI of the constitution, which stated: "no religious Test shall ever be required as a Qualification to any Office or public Trust under the United States." So, even the national frame was impaired by religious prejudice.

The American experiment did not succeed by force of words alone. It was aided by the spaciousness of the West and by immigration that created a more diverse population than the previous predominantly Protestant one. As Tocqueville accurately noted, the newly arrived Catholics were also among the staunchest defenders of religious freedom.

In the end, the national ethos was established by the commitment made in the constitution. The states eventually disestablished their established churches. A foreign observer like Tocqueville, anxious to hold up an example to his own countrymen, proclaimed the freedom of religion to be the distinctive mark of the American republic. Most importantly, religion was exercised freely and vigorously in the religionists' campaign for the abolition of slavery—a campaign subversive of the settled order, begun by Congregational ministers, carried on by a clerical network appealing to Christian duty, and reaching its culmination in a war whose battle hymn proclaimed, "God is marching on."

In these developments, the Supreme Court of the United States was a latecomer, having nothing to say on the state religious establishments or the abolitionists' campaign, except to reaffirm the constitution's acceptance of slavery. Even the enactment of the fourteenth amendment in 1868 did not alter the role of the court as bystander. The New Hampshire constitution, obnoxious as it was to religious liberty, was not altered until 1877 when demographic changes in New Hampshire made it no longer supportable.

The Supreme Court's one sustained venture in interpreting religious freedom after the Civil War was a series of cases involving the Church of Jesus Christ of Latter Day Saints. The Supreme Court, obedient to Congress's determination of the national interest, upheld a federal statute making polygamy criminal in the territories. The court also upheld a territorial statute that used a tried and true inquisitorial technique, an oath requiring the oath-swearer to disavow membership or belief in a church promoting polygamy as a doctrine. Climactically in 1890, the court enforced a federal law confiscating the property of the Mormon Church. In all these cases the court was reminded of the first amendment and, instead of heeding it, upheld the Christianity that the court found to have motivated the anti-Mormon legislation.

If one looked up "freedom, religious," in casebooks on constitutional law prior to the 1930s, the standard references were to the Mormon cases that rejected appeal to the first amendment. In the 1930s the Jehovah's Witnesses began to seek protection under the constitution. Jehovah's Witnesses believed that it was idolatry to salute the flag. They also believed in vigorous proselytizing. These beliefs, and the actions accompanying them, led to various state prosecutions. When the Witnesses appealed to the Supreme Court, they were rebuffed.

THE NEW INTERPRETER

Everything changed in 1940. The Supreme Court decided that religious liberty was a liberty protected from interference by the forty-eight states. The liberty was the free exercise of religion guaranteed by the first amendment. Not binding on the states originally, the first amendment was now incorporated by the Supreme Court into the fourteenth. Bystander no more, the court became a player.

The makers of the first amendment had never intended or anticipated that it would operate upon the states. The makers of the fourteenth amendment did have a sense that the religious freedom of the newly emancipated slaves needed protection from state action. But from 1868 to 1940 the states had not been held to a federal standard of free exercise.

What caused the change? As is true of many sudden alterations in constitutional doctrine by the Supreme Court, the court was reluctant to recognize the novelty, preferring not to acknowledge discontinuity, so the causes were not explicitly enumerated by the court itself. Three overlapping reasons for its action have been found. First, a doctrinal one going back to 1925: freedom of speech and freedom of the press as protected by the first amendment were read into the fourteenth amendment by the court. It was only a matter of time before religious freedom was moved in, too. The other two reasons go to timing. The Supreme Court had withdrawn from the business of invalidating governmental regulation of business. Courts abhor vacuums. Power unexercised is power gone. A new and vacant world of civil liberties lay open to supervision by judges with energy to spare for such action. At the same time, in the spring of 1940 the horror of Nazism loomed large in America. The Nazis' persecution of Jews was notorious. The time was ripe to assert the difference of the United States and to raise high the banner of religious freedom. The Supreme Court itself took note of the international context, referring in its opinion to the violence of those who acted "in the delusion of racial or religious conceit."

The court innovated on behalf of the beleaguered Jehovah's Witnesses, holding that their free exercise of religion had been restrained when Jesse Cantwell was prosecuted under a Connecticut statute requiring a charity to secure a license before soliciting money and under common law prohibiting breach of the peace. Both laws, it should be noted, were of a general character, not specifically aimed at Jehovah's Witnesses.

The implications of the innovation were not immediately digested by the court. In the same court term as *Cantwell*, the Supreme Court upheld the expulsion from public school in Pennsylvania of the children of Jehovah's Witnesses who refused to salute the flag. Writing for the court, Felix Frankfurter stressed that the Pennsylvania statute requiring salute of the flag was a general law that the legislature had deemed essential to secure an "orderly, tranquil, and free society." The statute required the salute "in the promotion of national cohesion." The court, Frankfurter went on, was dealing with "an interest inferior to none in the hierarchy of legal values. National unity is the basis of national security." The national interest in national security trumped the national invention of the free exercise of faith.

The decision drew a chorus of criticism from both the religious and the liberal secular press. Three years later, on Flag

Day, 1943, the court itself overruled this unfortunate precedent. Writing for the court in *Barnette* and extending protection to all beliefs, not only religious ones, Robert Jackson wrote: "If there is any fixed star in our constitutional constellation, it is that no official, high or petty, can prescribe what shall be orthodox in politics, nationalism, religion or other matters of opinion or force citizens to confess by word or act their faith therein." *Barnette* protected not merely opinion but the actual practice of refusing to obey a state statute compelling salute of the national symbol.

The flag salute statute was "of general applicability"; that is, it was not aimed as a weapon of persecution against Jehovah's Witnesses but prescribed the behavior of all children in the public schools of West Virginia. The general character of the statute did not save it. *Barnette* rhymed with *Cantwell* in finding the general applicability of a state statute no justification for enforcing it against persons whose religious scruples forbade them to obey. The high interest in national unity was no longer treated as a trump that permitted religious freedom to be abridged. In the midst of World War II, the free exercise of religion could not be prohibited for the sake of national security.

Cantwell and *Barnette*, high points in the early years of Supreme Court jurisprudence on religion, were complemented in 1972 by *Wisconsin v. Yoder*. The issue was whether the Old Order Amish had to obey the compulsory attendance law of the state and, against their religious beliefs, send their children to high school. The Amish did not offer alternative formal schooling; their position was that high school corrupted the religion of their children and endangered the salvation of the children and of the parents who sent them there. Chief Justice Burger, speaking for the court, observed: "Providing public schools ranks at the very apex of the function of a State." In this scale of values, the education of the citizens of a state stood with national unity as a prime governmental value. But higher than the highest function of the state was the constitutional freedom of parents to guide the religious future and education of their children.

The state of Wisconsin argued that free exercise extended only to belief, not actions, and that the compulsory school law was neutral in its application to all, whatever their religion. The court rejected both contentions. "[B]elief and action cannot be neatly confined in logic-tight compartments," the court observed. "[A] regulation neutral on its face" could "unduly burden the free exercise of religion." The exemption of the Amish from high school was required by the constitution. The exercise of the religion of the Amish by actual disobedience to the education laws of the state could not be prohibited.

Sixty years of free exercise jurisprudence have not always attained the level of *Cantwell*, *Barnette*, and *Yoder*. As may be unavoidable in the pull and tug of development of doctrine, there have been deviations and regressions. Although the first amendment spoke specifically only of *Congress* not enacting a law to restrict free exercise, the Supreme Court invariably enforced federal law over religious objections. States, municipalities, school boards were prevented from violating the first amendment. The national government was always found to have had a national interest that justified intrusion upon religious practice. If you were a legal realist, looking at what the Supreme Court did, rather than at what it said, you would conclude that free exercise was guaranteed against prohibition by every governmental unit except the United States itself.

THE BACKSLIDE OF 1990

In the course of development, a standard was set out by the court as to how intense the interest of the government had to be for the interest to trump free exercise. The governmental interest, the court said, had to be "compelling." Who was to decide if the interest was compelling? The court said it was for the court to decide. "Compelling interest," which does suggest a high measure of governmental need, could be dispensed with especially if the government was the federal government. For example, in 1988 the creation of a logging road by the United States Forest Service in a national forest was treated by the court as part of the ordinary operation of the federal government; the road could not be stopped even though it would cross the burial grounds of three Indian tribes, destroying "the Indians' ability to practice their religion." The compelling interest test was quietly set aside, although in theory it remained the criterion. The court did not seem to need to do more to assert its own supremacy.

Abruptly, in 1990, the court decided to change its announced criterion. The case involved the sacramental use of peyote by two members of the Native American Church. The two were fired by the private drug rehabilitation agency for which they worked. They applied for unemployment compensation. The state of Oregon denied it to them because they had engaged in misconduct, violating the drug laws of Oregon by their participation in the religious ingestion of peyote. They appealed to the Supreme Court, contending that the exercise of their religion was being prohibited by the state.

It would not have been a stretch to hold that Oregon had a compelling interest in supplementing its criminal laws against drugs by refusing aid to those who violated them. The litigants focused on the compelling interest. The court, however, took the case as the occasion for a major recasting of its jurisprudence on free exercise. It did so without even asking the litigants to brief the issue the court found dispositive.

The first amendment, the court announced, protected opinion and belief. Practice was another matter. Practice was not protected from laws "of general applicability" that incidentally had an impact upon the practice of a religion.

To achieve this result, the court had to put a new skin on old cases. In this way, *Cantwell* was explained as a free speech case where a license had unconstitutionally been required by the state. *Yoder* was said to have been decided on the basis of the right of parents to direct their children's education. Or, rather, both *Cantwell* and *Yoder* were analyzed as cases where the right of free exercise was bolstered by these other rights, the court speaking as if, by itself, free exercise would not have sufficed. One of the Mormon cases was treated as good precedent and invoked twice, although the antipolygamy laws had been squarely aimed at the Mormons' religion. Remarkably, *Barnette* was unmentioned. Instead, the opinion of Justice Frankfurter in the first flag salute case was rescued from oblivion and twice cited as though it had always been the law that conscientious practice of religion must bow to a statute of general applicability. Most surprising of all, the new opinion did not acknowledge that it was quoting an opinion overruled and repudiated by *Barnette*.

This change of course was not carried out without dissent as to the reasoning. Four justices contended that to reach its "sweeping result," the court had to "disregard our consistent application of free exercise doctrine to cases involving generally applicable regulations that burden religious conduct." The misreadings of *Cantwell* and of *Yoder* were tagged for what they were. Oddly enough, the court's reliance on an overruled opinion was let pass without particular notice. Over the dissent, five to four, the court retreated from Madison and reinstated the rule the Mormon cases had enforced. Belief could not be prohibited. Practice could, provided the law was general.

RFRA

The reaction to the peyote case, *Employment Division v. Smith*, united civil libertarians and many religious groups. A formidable and unusual coalition of the Left and the Right and the Center asked Congress to restore the old rule. Witnesses before Congress included the president of the American Civil Liberties Union, the chair of the People for the American Way Action Fund, and one of the Twelve Apostles of the Church of Jesus Christ of Latter Day Saints, as well as seasoned scholarly authorities on the first amendment, such as Robert Destro of the Catholic University of America, Edward M. Gaffney Jr., of Valparaiso Law School, and Douglas Laycock of the University of Texas.

Part of the testimony before Congress emphasized the shock of *Smith*, the sudden abandonment of established precedents, the extent of the damage likely to result, the insensitivity manifested to the requirements of conscience. The court's opinion in *Smith* had actually said that "we cannot afford the luxury of deeming presumptively invalid, as applied to the religious objector, every regulation of conduct that does not protect an interest of the higher order." Incredibly, it was remarked, free exercise was being characterized as a luxury. Other civil liberties secured by the first amendment would yield only to a compelling governmental interest. Why was free exercise treated as inferior? In the opinion of the president of the American Civil Liberties Union, *Smith* was "the *Dred Scott* of first amendment law." A variety of contemporary examples of laws of general application having actual or potential impact on the free exercise of religion were presented. It was pointed out that if *Smith* were good law and taken at its face in its quotation of Frankfurter, the broad freedom of conscience from compulsion established by *Barnette* no longer stood.

Congress responded. The House passed the Religious Freedom Restoration Act (RFRA) unanimously. The Senate passed it ninety-seven to three. President Clinton signed it into law on November 16, 1993. With its enactment Congress employed the power that the amendment of the constitution had granted it after the Civil War.

RFRA began with findings made by Congress that "laws 'neutral' toward religion may burden religious exercise as surely as laws intended to interfere with religious exercise" and that in *Smith* the Supreme Court had "virtually eliminated the requirement that the government justify burdens on religious exercise imposed by laws neutral toward religion." Having set out its target, RFRA provided: "Government shall not substantially burden a person's exercise of religion even if the burden results from a rule of general applicability except...." The exception was where the burden imposed was "in furtherance of a compelling governmental interest" and "the least restrictive means" were used to further that interest.

RFRA was designed as legislation appropriate to enforce the provision of section 1 of the fourteenth amendment, guarantee-

ing that no person shall be arbitrarily deprived of liberty by a
state. The fourteenth amendment, section 1 declares:

> No State shall make or enforce any law which shall abridge
> the privileges or immunities of citizens of the United States,
> nor shall any State deprive any person of life, liberty or
> property without due process of law, nor deny to any per-
> son within its jurisdiction the equal protection of the laws.

Section 5 of the fourteenth amendment states:

> The Congress shall have power to enforce, by appropriate
> legislation, the provisions of this article.

Congress exercised the power conferred on it by section 5 "to enforce" the amendment's provisions "by appropriate legislation."

In 1940 in *Cantwell*, the Supreme Court by reading the first
amendment into the fourteenth had taken upon itself the definition of the liberty protected by section 1 of the fourteenth. Section 1 was a very broad prohibition. If it was to be more than
an empty exhortation, it had to be applied to particular acts of
deprivation. It had to be given effect, it had to be enforced. The
Supreme Court in 1940 had not only defined liberty but enforced the protection of it. Not before RFRA had Congress
exercised as to religious liberty the power to enforce conferred
upon it by section 5. When Congress finally used the power the
constitution gave it and, doing so, explicitly rebuked the Supreme Court, would the court accept the rebuke?

The court's view, to be expressed in *Boerne*, was that the guarantees of life, liberty, and property in section 1 of the fourteenth
amendment are "self-executing." But no law, no constitution is
"self-executing." Lawyers, judges, marshals, process servers are
all required to make any provision of law come to life. When

the court described this portion of the constitution as "self-executing," the court unselfconsciously identified the court with the constitution. The guarantees were "self-executing" in the sense that the court would execute them, and the assumption was made that the court and the constitution were the same.

The Congress that drafted the fourteenth amendment after the Civil War had been deeply suspicious of the Supreme Court, still under a cloud for its notorious decision in *Dred Scott*. *Dred Scott* had denied congressional power to prevent slavery extending into the territories governed by federal law; had denied the very possibility of any descendant of a slave becoming a citizen of the United States; and, by its maladroit effort to end the controversy over slavery with a kind of final solution sustaining it forever, had helped bring on the Civil War. The drafters of the fourteenth amendment did not desire to destroy a federal structure or concentrate all power in Congress. Still less, however, did they have in mind a grant of power to the court. They gave power for the amendment's enforcement to Congress.

In 1879, eleven years after the states had ratified the amendment, the Supreme Court, now dominated by Northern Republicans, had occasion to examine its scope. Disavowing power in the judicial branch to enforce or to protect the rights guaranteed, the court in *Ex parte Virginia* declared:

> It is the power of Congress which has been enlarged....
> Whatever legislation is appropriate, that is, adapted to carry
> out the objects the amendments have in view, whatever
> tends to enforce submission to the prohibitions they contain,
> and to secure to all persons the enjoyment of perfect equali-
> ty of civil rights and the equal protection of the laws against

State denial or invasion, if not prohibited, is brought within the domain of congressional power.

The words of section 5 granting Congress power to enact "appropriate" laws were even broader than the words of article I, section 8 of the constitution that empowered Congress to legislate on commerce, crime, currency, and other federal matters. There the empowering language spoke of legislation that was "necessary and proper." These two terms arguably constituted a restraint, leaving to a court the determination of what federal laws met the conjoint criteria of being both needed and proper. Did Congress have power to create a national bank? Not a word in the constitution addressed the question. But when Congress had exercised its article I, section 8 power to create the Bank of the United States, and Maryland attempted to tax the bank, Chief Justice John Marshall had held that Congress had acted within its powers, creating a bank that was not only national but by implication free from taxation by the states. In *McCulloch v. Maryland*, Marshall wrote:

> Let the end be legitimate, let it be within the scope of the
> constitution, and all means which are appropriate, which
> are plainly adapted to that end, which are not prohibited,
> but consist with the letter and spirit of the constitution,
> are constitutional.

So, "necessary and proper" had been expanded to "appropriate," and "appropriate" had been explained to include what was adapted to an end within the powers conferred on Congress. The drafters of the fourteenth amendment used the talismanic term of *McCulloch*—"appropriate"—to describe the amplitude of power that the amendment conferred on Congress.

Civil rights legislation in the 1960s had relied on this amplitude to override the Supreme Court. In 1959, the court had held that a test of literacy in English imposed by North Carolina did not violate the fourteenth amendment even when the test was used to disqualify African Americans as voters. Congress had responded with the Voting Rights Act of 1965, prohibiting such testing of anyone who had passed the sixth grade. The protection of the new law was sought by Puerto Ricans living in New York. The state of New York defended the English literacy requirement, a part of its constitution since 1916. The state contended that the Supreme Court had already determined the constitutionality of such a requirement in its 1959 decision for North Carolina, and that Congress was powerless to change the court's understanding of the constitution.

The Supreme Court cited and quoted both the 1879 case of *Ex parte Commonwealth of Virginia* and Marshall's opinion in *McCulloch v. Maryland* and, in terms of both cases, explained the power given Congress to enforce the fourteenth amendment. The evidence that Congress was remedying purposeful discrimination against Puerto Ricans was slight. There were not many immigrants from Puerto Rico to New York in 1916 when the literacy test had been enacted. The court put in a footnote the evidence it said Congress might have had. The evidence consisted in quotation of a single statement made at the New York State Constitutional Convention of 1916 that there was danger to "our race" if literacy in English was not required for voters. The Supreme Court also noted, without further elaboration, "the cultural milieu" from 1915 to 1921 as "evidence" of which Congress was aware. The Voting Rights Act of 1965, finding a freedom whose existence the Supreme Court had denied seven years earlier, was held to be constitutional. The Voting Rights Act precedent, the ample implications of section 5's "appropriate," and the equivalence of section 5 power to the article I power so broadly construed by John Marshall, all pointed to the full legitimacy of RFRA. Those who relied on such pledges by the Supreme Court did not consider sufficiently that the court could change its mind.

A CHURCH DIVIDED, A VILLAGE SPLIT, A CONSTITUTION REMADE

Boerne, a city in Texas parlance, was a village of a little over four thousand inhabitants, located twenty-five miles from San Antonio. It possessed a single Catholic church, St. Peter the Apostle. The parish was formed in the 1860s when a determined French missionary had built for German immigrants a small church on a hill on the outskirts of the settlement. This structure was preserved when a larger edifice was begun in 1923, modeled after Mission Concepcion in San Antonio. In 1991, a new pastor, Father Tony Cummings, was assigned to St. Peter's by Patrick Flores, archbishop of San Antonio. Father Cummings's assignment was to enlarge the church of the 1920s to accommodate a growing congregation. He counted 780 families enrolled in the parish. The church seated 250 persons. Even when he arranged for three masses on Sundays, the people were, in his words, squeezed in "like sardines." There were often thirty or more standing. The need for space was undeniable. The question was how to obtain it.

In 1991 Father Cummings took advice and began to plan a new church, leaving intact little more than the twin bell towers that marked the main entrance of the 1923 edifice. In the same year, not coincidentally, the city council of Boerne adopted an ordinance designed to preserve buildings in what it designated as "an historic district." St. Peter's, or part of it, fell within the district. Anna Marie Davison, a member of the parish and a leading preservationist, pressed the Texas Historical Commission to give the church landmark status and prevent its alteration. She did not succeed with the state commission, but she roused the town. A battle that would divide the parish and the town began.

Few issues, it may be observed, are more likely to rouse local passions than disputes over zoning. The natural sense of the owners of the property, that they should be allowed to do what they want with what they own, is put in conflict with the community's sense that property rights are not absolute and that there is a communal interest in congruence, history, or aesthetics that may need to be taken into account. The conflict is intensified when the zoning is focused on preservation of a building that the owners no longer find useful. Why should they who built it be forced to keep it at their expense? A fortiori, the question is pressed when the building is a church put up as a place to worship and no longer able to accommodate the worshippers. In Europe, governments take on the cost of the upkeep of historic shrines. In America, local governments, often enough, would like the churches to shoulder the burden. Is forced preservation of an unusable structure a type of prohibition of religion?

Feelings ran high. The majority of the congregation backed Cummings. He got over $600,000 in pledges to do the remodeling when he would be permitted to do it. Still, a minority, mostly old-time members of the parish, stirred by Anna Marie Davison, steadfastly opposed the plans for change. The new design was denounced as nondescript, a destruction of beauty, a horror. The archbishop and then the pope were asked to intervene to stop the desecration. The rest of the town joined the battle. It was questioned whether the zone of the Historic District embraced more than the bell towers, which the parish promised to preserve. Finally, the Historic Landmarks Commission of Boerne, the local body charged with enforcing the zoning of the Historic District, denied the church a permit to go ahead with demolition. In the spring of 1994, after a tense public hearing, the city council, four to one, sustained the denial of the license. Cummings, describing the outcome as "morally and grossly unjust," moved Sunday masses to the Rainbow Senior Citizens' Center. Archbishop Flores entered the scene, seeking relief under RFRA in the federal district court in Midland, Texas. No compelling governmental interest, he maintained, justified Boerne's burden imposed upon the believers.

In February 1995, Boerne raised as a defense to Flores's suit a challenge to the constitutionality of RFRA. The solicitor general of the United States entered the case to defend the legislation. In March 1995, District Judge Lucius Desha Bunton III held RFRA unconstitutional. He quoted John Marshall: "It is emphatically the province and duty of the judicial department to say what the law is." Departing from the Supreme Court's position in the peyote case, Congress had violated the constitution.

Appeal was taken to the court of appeals for the Fifth Circuit sitting in New Orleans. The panel to whom the case was fortuitously assigned was composed of Patrick E. Higginbotham,

Emilio Garza, and Fortunado Benavides. The panel's composition was chiefly of importance in reflecting a broad range of backgrounds and experience. On January 23, 1996, in an opinion by Higginbotham, the panel unanimously reversed Judge Bunton.

Applying Supreme Court precedent, the court of appeals noted three questions to be answered: First, might RFRA be regarded as an enactment to enforce the protection of religious freedom, guaranteed from infringement by the state? Citing the testimony of three witnesses before the House of Representatives, the court found it easy to answer the question affirmatively. Second, was RFRA "plainly adapted" to the purpose of enforcement? The court noted that Congress had no power to add to the fourteenth amendment but did have power to act remedially "where a violation lurks." As the United States now argued, RFRA supplied a remedy to facially neutral laws actually hostile to religious exercise; acted prophylactically in preventing such laws; and aided religious minorities, such as the Amish, Hmong, Jewish, and Mormon, that had suffered because their religious practices had not been respected by the majority. The third question was whether RFRA was consistent with the letter and spirit of the constitution. Unquestionably, it was. The city argued that Congress had usurped the power of the Supreme Court. The answer was given by the Voting Rights case. As it had with voting rights, Congress could go beyond the bare constitutional minimum. The Supreme Court in the peyote case had not held that a law exempting religious exercise from statutes of general applicability was unconstitutional; all the court had decided was that exemption was not required. Now Congress had lawfully gone beyond this minimum.

The Supreme Court granted certiorari in *Boerne*. The same lawyers who had faced each other in New Orleans argued in Washington—Douglas Laycock, a leading authority on the constitution and religious liberty, appearing for the archbishop, and Marci Hamilton, a young professor at Cardozo Law School in New York, representing Boerne. Walter Dellinger, solicitor general of the United States, argued on the archbishop's side, reflecting RFRA's popularity with the Clinton administration and the judgment of the executive branch that RFRA's restrictions would not seriously restrict the federal government. Argued in February 1997, the case was decided in June at the end of the court's term.

The court's starting point was that the power of Congress under section 5 of the fourteenth amendment was remedial. Congress could act to cure an evil. It could not act to enlarge the rights the amendment guaranteed. Admittedly, the line between a remedy and the creation of an enlarged right was "not easy to discern." Admittedly, Congress "must have wide latitude in determining where it [the line] lies." But, the court reassured itself, "the distinction exists and must be observed."

How was the distinction to be observed? Here the court unveiled a new test for legislation: "There must be a congruence and proportionality between the injury to be prevented or remedied and the means adopted to that end." This formula was unprecedented. Proportionality in legislation! Who would measure the proportion? Implicitly, the answer was "the court." What measure would the court use? Implicitly, the answer was "whatever we find handy." A few years earlier, scorn had been heaped by members of the court themselves on the notion of the court measuring proportionality in criminal sentences. How would the court know, two justices had asked, what proportion should be observed? A determination of proportionality between a crime and its punishment, according to these members of the court, invited the "imposition of subjective judgment." If objective measures did not aid in an area where common sense had at least some competence, what measure could the court use when determining the proportion between violations of civil rights and laws meant to cure or prevent such violations? Was there anything but subjective feeling for the justices to use as a measuring stick?

Introduction of the test introduced a judicial concern with the record upon which Congress acted. When the question had been, Is the law remedial?, it had been enough for a court to see that Congress had been aware of evils in need of elimination or prevention. When congruence and proportionality were the measures, there appeared to be a need for a court to look more closely at what evils the legislation was said to be eliminating or preventing.

The Supreme Court looked more closely at the record made in the legislative hearings on RFRA. The court observed that there had been "anecdotal evidence of autopsies performed on Jewish individuals and Hmong immigrants in violation of their religious beliefs." The court observed that there had been testimony to the "adverse effects" of zoning and preservation laws on churches and synagogues. The court discounted this evidence because the examples did not evince a governmental purpose to discriminate against religion. The burdens imposed were "incidental." No religious persecution by law had been shown to have occurred "in the past 40 years."

Measured by this evidence, paltry and unconvincing as the evidence in the court's eyes was, RFRA was overkill. RFRA's "sweeping coverage" assured "its intrusion at every level of government." RFRA applied "to every agency and official" of federal, state, and local government. It had no termination date. Its protections could be invoked by any individual who alleged that an action of the government burdened his or her religion. It was disproportionate to the evils established by the record.

In *Cantwell v. Connecticut* in 1940 the Supreme Court on the basis of the record in a single case had created a new rule of law binding all fifty states. Congress, acting on the basis of legislative hearings, testimony by experts, and accounts of oppression by individuals, was now declared by the court not to have enough evidence of discrimination against religion to fashion a law setting a standard of proof of such discrimination.

The court did not pause to note that the sweep of RFRA paralleled the sweep of the first amendment. It, too, had been interpreted by the court itself to bind all units of government. It, too, had no termination date. It, too, could be invoked by an individual. The court's real quarrel with RFRA was that RFRA made incidental burdens on free exercise provable as substantial burdens that prohibited free exercise in violation of the first amendment. The court's position was that only purposeful persecution constituted prohibition. For the court the case was as simple as that. The court had already spoken. Congress could not enlarge the liberty protected.

An alternative approach, also fatal to RFRA, was attractive to one member of the majority. Any exemption for religion from a general law was, in this member's view, an establishment of religion. Establishment of a religion was forbidden by the same amendment that protected free exercise. Protection of free exercise, therefore, could not extend to exemptions.

The difficulty of this position was that, if applied, it would clash with a variety of particular exemptions created by Congress, some of them already accepted by the Supreme Court. Most notable were the exemptions for clergy, persons studying for the ministry, and conscientious objectors to all war—exemptions made by the draft laws in both World War I and World War II. After the nineteenth amendment prohibited the sale of liquor "for beverage purposes," Congress in the Volstead Act had permitted the sale of liquor for the purpose of being consumed in religious services, such as those held by Catholics, Episcopalians, Jews, and Lutherans. If the wine was consumed, it was used as a beverage; but the statute was evidently allowed to amend the constitution. After the Supreme Court had held that the Old Order Amish were not entitled to an exemption from Social Security by reason of their religious belief, Congress gave them one. After the Supreme Court had held that the free exercise of religion did not entitle an Orthodox Jew to wear a yarmulke when he was on duty as an officer of the Air Force, Congress had created the exemption. After the Supreme Court had refused to stop the logging road through Indian burial grounds, Congress stopped it. If all these exemptions were bad as establishments of religion, a more wholesale revision of the laws would have to be undertaken than the court contemplated.

Unless exemption was establishment, the issue of all the exemptions from federal law was not presented by *Boerne*. It was remarkable then that in computing the disproportionate sweep of RFRA, the court should have added RFRA's impact on all federal laws and agencies to its calculation. That Congress had the power to restrict federal law from prohibiting the exercise of religion had never been doubted by the court as a whole.

All the exemptions Congress had made, now unmentioned by the court, stood as mute testimony to the long standing belief of the legislative and executive branches as to the respect to be accorded free exercise. The exceptions also stood as testimony to the workability of exceptions. If great federal bureaucracies could live with them, couldn't city hall? But this question was not addressed. No doubt the exceptions were also evidence that large minorities (as in the case of sacramental wine) or small but strategically knowledgeable minorities (as in the case of Social Security or the case of the yarmulke) could secure exceptions without judicial help. So why should the judiciary bother itself? This way of thinking had been explicit in the court's opinion in *Smith*. The answer, as obvious as the question, was that the most odious kind of anomaly was not an exception to the law but judicial indifference to a right the other branches of government believed that the constitution secured.

The court's way of handling this anomaly was not to address it but to announce the new tests—variously phrased as "congruence and proportionality" or as "congruence or proportionality"—and the consequent scrutiny by the court of the evidence Congress had considered. Unnecessary in reaching the result, the new tests carried what in modern jargon was the metamessage of *Boerne* addressed to Congress: Six or even five of us count for more than five hundred of you because the constitution has provided us with a province and a function in regard to federal legislation, a duty to give definitive meaning to the foundational document. We are not to be governed by the judgments made by the two branches of government that are our co-equals but that are not equal to us in the discharge of this duty. Performing it, we are not only the highest court in the land but the highest authority. Our words constitute the constitution that is now in force.

Conveying that message, the court created, for possible future use against Congress, two new and powerful weapons to be deployed in constitutional litigation: that the congressional record could be closely inspected for convincing evidence of the evil legislated against, and that the legislation responding to the evil must be congruent or proportionate or both. The test of "congruence and proportionality" was unchallenged by any member of the court. One of the three dissenters explicitly agreed with it. The absence of challenge to the creation of new criteria vitally affecting the balance between the courts and Congress was an unusual characteristic of the case.

The battle in Boerne was over. After the court's decision, villagers asked, "Who's in charge—Congress or the Supreme Court?" and grumbled audibly about being made pawns in a test case. Both sides professed to be ready to fight on. But a compromise was soon reached. A new remodeling plan kept 80 percent of the 1923 church and won a national architectural award. Father Cummings got seven hundred more seats. The real battle begun by *Boerne* was to continue. Were the new requirements for legislation ad hoc defenses set up by the Supreme Court to rebuff RFRA or would they be norms governing the future? *Boerne* raised this question without resolving it. Resolution of this question was to interact with the immunity the court attributed to sovereigns.

CHAPTER 2

Superior Beings

Samuel Simple, a federal appellate judge in San Francisco, had completed his pilgrim's process in the intricate forest of the first amendment as it touches on religion when he encountered the cases of the past five years restricting the power of federal law and invalidating new and old acts of Congress. The cases seemed to him to turn on a concept that had not been very prominent when he had gone to law school in the 1960s.

As Simple thought about the cases, he observed to his law clerks, "There's a background factor that's at work that I have to understand. It's the immunity from suit that a state enjoys because the states are sovereigns. I suppose it's a matter of constitutional law."

"There is nothing in the constitution about it," Yalewoman broke in. "Neither sovereignty nor immunity is so much as mentioned."

"State immunity wasn't a factor either in *Boerne*, which is a key part of the whole shift," observed Boaltman. "The Supreme Court talked broadly about RFRA's burden on the states, as though Texas was a defendant. But as you know well, judge, the defendant in *Boerne* was a village. The state of Texas wasn't affected."

"Well, I'm wrong on two counts," Simple sighed, "but I do think it's in the background of all these cases, and I do have the impression that some justices put the doctrine on a par with the constitution. Why don't we start by your telling me what the rule is today?"

"Very well, judge," Harvardman weighed in. "The law today is that each of the fifty states is a sovereign, and a sovereign cannot be sued for damages by an individual, an Indian tribe, or a foreign government unless the sovereign has consented to being sued. An unconsenting state, therefore, cannot be sued in federal court or in state court except by the federal government itself. It cannot be sued even though Congress in the exercise of the powers conferred by article I has given individuals the right to sue. Its immunity from private suits is, as the court has expressed it, 'central to sovereign dignity.'"

"Name the cases establishing the modern law," said Simple.

"As to foreign countries, it was *Monaco* in 1934; as to Indian tribes, it was *Blatchford* in 1991," recited Harvardman. "*Seminole Tribe* in 1996 made clear that Congress in the exercise of a power given it under article I could not pierce the states' immunity. *Alden* in 1999 held that the unconsenting state was as immune in its own courts as it was in the federal system.

"Of those four, it's been *Seminole* that cut deeply into the powers of Congress over the fifty states. 'Even where the Constitution vests in Congress complete lawmaking authority over a particular area,' the court declared, the states cannot be made liable for damages when they violate federal law."

"In a word," added Boaltman, "*Seminole* is seminal."

"That seems simple," Simple said. "But isn't there any connection between immunity and the constitution?"

"It's inherent in the constitution," Harvardman said tersely. "At least the Supreme Court says it's 'inherent' or 'implicit.'"

"For the present," Simple nodded, "we need not go beyond the court's teaching. We can go back to its reasoning later. But I'm still puzzled about the law. Every day I'm dealing with habeas corpus petitions of state prisoners asking me to order the warden to release the prisoner who says he's being held in violation of federal law. Isn't the sovereign state the real defendant in these habeas cases? What is more important to a sovereign than custody of its criminals?"

"I did answer you in formal terms, judge," replied Harvardman. "Of course, there is an exception to immunity. What rule of law does not have an exception? I should have gone on to say habeas actions have always been viewed as actions against the individual state officer, not against the sovereign. The state is not a party on the record."

"It's certainly the real party in interest," Simple observed. "The state has decided to indict the prisoner and to prosecute him. A state's court has convicted him, and its appellate courts have confirmed his conviction. The attorney general of the state is defending his incarceration. The warden—the nominal respondent—doesn't have any personal interest in keeping him imprisoned. It is the state that says this man has violated its laws and must be punished. Even the briefs in the federal habeas case drop the fiction that the case is against the warden. The briefs say, 'The state argues,' 'California maintains,' etc. No one, not for one minute, thinks the state is not before the federal judge hearing the habeas petition.

"A fortiori, that's true when the state has exercised the most fundamental of sovereign prerogatives, the power of life or death, and sentenced a prisoner to die. The highest court of the state will have reviewed the case at least once, maybe two or three times. The governor will have been asked for clemency and will have denied it. The state will have announced the date and hour of execution. The prison will have prepared the death chamber. It is not any individual who then impugns the state's dignity by bringing his case before a federal court, but the most miserable individual, a man judged to be a murderer, an outcast from civil society. Yet a single federal district judge at the instance of this individual can tell the state that it is wrong, its proceedings have been in vain, and the execution must stop. Where is the immunity of the state when it would be most supportive of the state's status as a sovereign?"

The law clerks were silent before this outburst of the judge, who after a moment asked, "Is easy fiction acceptable only in habeas or does it have a wider application?"

"All *Ex parte Young*–type cases are an exception," Yalewoman chimed in. "You remember the facts. Minnesota set rates for railroads within its jurisdiction that stockholders of the railroads challenged as the unconstitutional taking of their property. They also challenged the criminal penalties—the heavy fines threatened by the statute for any railroad and the incarceration threatened for any railroad agent disobeying the new rates. The criminal penalties acted *in terrorem* to discourage any disobedience. The stockholders got a federal injunction against Edward T. Young, attorney general of Minnesota, forbidding him to enforce the criminal law. Young disobeyed the injunction. The federal district court held him in contempt and ordered his imprisonment. His appeal reached the Supreme Court of the United States. Young argued that the injunction had been invalid because it had attempted to bind the sovereign state of Minnesota in the execution of its criminal law. The Supreme Court held that the Minnesota law was unconstitutional. The injunction only bound him, Edward T. Young. When an officer of the state sought to enforce an unconstitutional law, he was 'stripped' of his official status. He became just a lawless individual fully subject to coercion by the federal court upholding the constitution. Now, officers of the states are all the time being sued for unconstitutional takings and being told by federal judges to change their ways.

"This simple dodge works wonders," she added. "Before *Seminole* anyway, the state officers could be hauled into federal court not only for taking your property but for treading on the snail darter or some similar creature near extinction that Congress had elected to protect and to prefer to the state. If it is supposed to be beneath the state's dignity to be sued by an individual, imagine the loss of dignity when the real party of interest is a whale. Moby Dick may still be able to sue the Massachusetts Director of Fisheries for violating the Endangered Species Act."

"Stripping an officer of his status—that sounds almost violent," Judge Simple mused. "But I see that it does the trick. Ordinarily I suppose all the individual plaintiff has to do is *allege* that the state action is unconstitutional. Until the federal court tries the case, it doesn't know whether the law is actually invalid. The allegation will be enough to leave the state official vulnerable to suit."

"You're right there, judge," said Boaltman. "But there is an exception to this exception. If the officer is sued for money damages because of some unconstitutional act he has performed for the state, he keeps his official status. The suit for money is a suit against the state. The state is immune."

"What a serviceable fiction!" the judge exclaimed. "Half the time it will work and half the time it won't. What a masterly compromise that lets plaintiffs stop unconstitutional state action and prevents plaintiffs from being reimbursed for it!"

"It does seem, intuitively speaking, to work just the wrong way round," Yalewoman observed. "If you were going to provide immunity by a half, wouldn't it make more sense to say that an ongoing project of the state could not be halted by a litigious individual, but if the state was found in fact to have violated a constitutional right that it should make up for the damage it has caused? That way, you wouldn't let important work be interrupted but the states would be on notice that they would have to pay if they were mistaken.

"If you can't get damages from a state, then action by a state officer that damages you inflicts injury that's irreparable. Irreparable injury is ground for an injunction against the state officer. That may tie up the state more than paying damages would."

"It's no good trying to redo a century of precedent," said Boaltman. "And there's another curious quirk in the way the fiction is used. According to the Supreme Court in *Pennhurst*, if the state officer has only violated state law, the fiction won't be applied. The fiction is there only to aid in enforcement of federal law. State immunity is one of those things that are a little bit magical. Now you don't see it, now you do."

"Besides the magic, there's more than a small difficulty with *Ex parte Young* and its progeny," Harvardman interjected. "The basis for any federal intervention in a case like *Young* is that *the state* is taking property without due process of law. What is alleged is a violation of the fourteenth amendment, and the fourteenth amendment forbids states to do such things. The fourteenth amendment does not apply to individuals. To get the injunction against Young it was necessary to say that through him the state was acting. So, in the same case, a person is considered for legal purposes to be the state and is considered for legal purposes not to be the state. Can that be done without violating the laws of logic and the principle of contradiction that says A cannot be X and not X at the same time?"

"It's a logical mess," Yalewoman responded, "and it's really intolerable. How can people have respect for a system that violates the laws of logic in one of the system's most important operations?"

"You know," said Boaltman, "the problem has been spotted by the justices. Some of them have called it 'a well-recognized irony,' but an irony that must be perpetuated because 'the rule of *Ex parte Young* is one of the cornerstones of the Court's Eleventh Amendment jurisprudence.'"

"Irony!" Yalewoman exclaimed. "The real irony is that a formal oxymoron should be a cornerstone of the jurisprudence of any court."

"People don't know or don't think about it," Simple remarked. "We've lived with it almost a century, ever since *Ex parte Young* was decided in 1908. As long as we know what we're doing, does it hurt to say, 'Let's pretend the attorney general is not the state when we enjoin him, while we enjoin him precisely because he is the state'?"

"It only hurts when you think about it," Yalewoman tactlessly replied.

"Anyway, there are members of the court who would like to take a big bite out of *Ex parte Young*," Boaltman noted. "The court itself agrees that it's just an 'obvious fiction' to provide a federal forum on some occasions, so two members of the court now say 'a careful balancing and accommodation of state interest' must be undertaken to determine if *Ex parte Young* applies. For them, it's a 'case-by-case approach.' When a suit affected Idaho's ownership of water resources or its ability to regulate Coeur d'Alene Lake, all defendants were held to be immune, even though they included Larry Echohawk, attorney general of the state, and Keith Higginson, the director of the department of water resources, both personally sued just like Edward T. Young."

"All fiction aside, there's a formal exemption," Harvardman added. "When Congress appropriately exercises its power under section 5 of the fourteenth amendment, Congress does create a right enforceable against a state. That is because the fourteenth amendment did transfer certain powers from the states to the federal government."

"We now know there are three exceptions to the immunity that the court says is 'central to sovereign dignity,'" Simple noted. "The state can be brought into federal court at the instance of an individual filing a habeas petition or alleging an unconstitutional taking or claiming a right under a federal law abrogating the state's immunity by virtue of section 5 of the fourteenth amendment. Are we missing any exception?"

"One is staring us in the face, judge," exclaimed Boaltman. "The Supreme Court of the United States has the power to review decisions by state courts where the constitution or a federal law is involved. The decision of the highest court of the state will be subjected to examination and possible reversal when the Supreme Court exercises its power. Realistically, what could have more impact on a sovereign's dignity than to have its highest tribunal reversed by another court?"

"There's a second angle to the Supreme Court's appellate jurisdiction here," Harvardman stated. "Review of the supreme court of a state by the Supreme Court happens whether or not the state itself is a litigant. But even when the state itself is the litigant, it can be brought into the national forum. Suppose the state has consented to be sued in its own courts. If the state then is a defendant by consent and the case turns on a federal question, its consent becomes, willy-nilly, consent to the Supreme Court of the United States adjudicating its contentions. Similarly, if the state is the plaintiff in such a case, it may find the national tribunal finally determining its case without its consent."

"Even before a state case gets to the Supreme Court," Boaltman added, "the case can be removed from the state court to a federal district court if the person the state is suing can show that federal law preempts the state law. Willy-nilly again, the state must then subject itself to the federal judiciary."

"That makes a total of six exceptions to immunity if you count Supreme Court review of state supreme court decisions," Simple calculated. "Is there a seventh?"

"The United States itself can always sue a state," reported Boaltman. "It's in effect the sovereign of the fifty sovereigns. The latter have no dignity to shield them from the boss sovereign."

"Now that we know that the states have immunity with seven exceptions, what more do I need to know?" Simple inquired.

"What is a state," Yalewoman responded. "Towns, cities, counties are not states; neither are school boards, regional authorities, or redevelopment authorities. At least they are not for purposes of immunity. If the governmental activities of an agency embrace the whole state, it will probably be identified with the state."

"Does the agency have to carry the designation 'State' in its title to qualify?" Simple asked.

"No," said Boaltman. "The University of California has the immunity of the state without carrying 'State' in its name. A tug on the Erie Canal turned out to have the state's immunity when the tug's lessee was the state of New York."

"It surprises me a little," Simple commented. "A great city like Los Angeles has none of the prerogatives of sovereignty, while a branch of the University of California is treated as identical with the sovereign state or, in judicial-speak, as 'an arm of the state.' Can the state multiply its immunity by multiplying its arms or agencies?"

"The line hasn't yet been drawn," Boaltman replied. "But it's clear that modern American states create agencies unknown in earlier days, and the agencies get the states' immunity. A lot more immune governmental bodies exist now than ever before. They are engaged in everything from building bridges and roads to running hospitals and colleges. The creations of the state covered by the mantle of the state are many. In California, for example, there are the Barbering and Cosmetology Program; the California School for the Blind; the California School for the Deaf; the Horse Racing Board; and the Lottery—all agencies of the state.

"There's one further wrinkle worth noting," Boaltman continued, "even though it's only the court's construction of a statute. One of the most effective federal remedies for deprivation of a civil right is provided by the civil rights legislation that permits suits against 'persons' who, under color of state law, deprive you of a constitutional right. Under this statute, so the Supreme Court has held, a city is a 'person,' but a state is not, neither is an agency of the state, neither is an official of the state acting officially. The reason for this result, according to the court, is that 'in common usage' a sovereign is not a person. An official of the state sued as an official is cloaked by the sovereign's lack of personhood. Hence African-American state police officers could not sue the Department of Public Safety of the state of Michigan nor its Director of State Police for discriminating against them. The department and its director were not persons. The decision has added to the fortifications protecting the states."

"Here's another anomaly," Yalewoman contributed. "Cities and counties are not states for purposes of immunity, but they are treated as states for purposes of enforcing the civil rights acts, which are enacted under the fourteenth amendment. The fourteenth amendment, we have been repeatedly told by the court, applies only to the states, yet the civil rights acts do not apply to the states but do apply to bodies that are not states. And the local bodies are treated as persons.

"It's not the same kind of logical error committed in *Ex parte Young*," Yalewoman added. "That's a blunder in logic. Here there's simple inconsistency. The Supreme Court says the fourteenth amendment applies only to states, but forgets this saying and applies legislation under the amendment to units of government that no one pretends are states.

"Sometimes the court seems to delight in puzzling paradoxes, as if to stimulate the ingenuity of constitutional law professors. The court speaks of 'our longstanding interpretive presumption that "person" does not include the sovereign.' At the same time the court declares, 'We have long recognized that a State's sovereign immunity is "a personal privilege which it may waive at pleasure."' Dignity and personal privileges seem to be what persons possess, but the court insists that the state is no person."

"It's odd," Harvardman observed, "that the relative pronoun that goes most readily with 'sovereign' is 'who,' not 'which.' Could we have come upon more than an anomaly—in fact, upon another oxymoron, a personal privilege of a nonperson?"

None of the group appeared ready to refute this suggestion or to pursue the court's conundrums further.

"Perhaps now that we know the breadth of immunity, we should look at its rationale," Simple proposed. "After all, there must be a reason for every law, and the scope of the law should not go beyond the reason for its existence."

"*Cessante ratione, cessat ipsa lex,*" Harvardman interjected, adding, "As the canonists put it, when the reason for the law ceases, so does the law. The reason articulated by the Supreme Court has a rather abstract character. It is that being sued without consent impairs the dignity of the state. You remember that the court has said that the founding fathers considered immunity from private suits 'central to sovereign dignity.'"

"I can't believe it," Yalewoman broke in indignantly. "I can't believe that you, or the court itself, take this kind of guff seriously."

"I won't answer for myself," said Harvardman, "but as far as the court is concerned and as far as its words can be taken at face value, the dignity of each of the fifty states is on its mind as a thing to be jealously guarded."

"What kind of thing do you imagine the court thinks dignity is?" Yalewoman snorted. "You can't eat it, touch it, feel it. To be a little more philosophical, isn't it a tautology? The states have immunity, therefore the states have dignity. You can reverse it: The states have dignity, therefore they have immunity. Immunity and dignity say the same thing. Dignity is not an explanation why immunity is granted."

"I must admit I've had misgivings, too," Harvardman rejoined. "I've thought about the question why it should be a loss of dignity to be sued without consent. Any one of us as individuals can be sued without asking our permission. Do we lose dignity when we respond to a summons or answer a complaint? I have never thought so or heard anyone ever say so."

"Blackstone has the answer, judge," said Yalewoman a trifle caustically. "He was the prime authority on the common law for our founders, and he tells us exactly what the dignity of the sovereign is and why it's called for. The king, he says, has dignity because 'it is necessary to distinguish a prince from his subjects, not only by the outward pomp and decorations of majesty, but also by ascribing to him certain qualities, as inherent in his royal capacity, distinct from and superior to those of any other individual in the nation.' Therefore, the law ascribes to the king 'certain attributes of a great and transcendent nature; by which the people are led to consider him in the light of a superior being, and to pay him that awful respect, which may enable him with greater ease to carry on the burden of government.'"

"I guess a king might have dignity and lose it if made to appear in person before a judge he himself had appointed," conceded Harvardman, "but a modern bureaucrat? No one supposes that the governor of even a great state like California is a superior being, and I doubt if any would be willing to think of the state itself as one."

"Note, too," Boaltman chimed in, "the seven exceptions where the state can be made to answer. Some of these exceptions are quite common. If being made to respond to pleading in a federal court diminishes dignity, the states daily lose dignity by the yard or the pound or whatever measure applies to such an intangible and imperceptible quality."

"I see you young people don't put much store in a fine old term that I suspect must have theological roots," observed the judge. "I must ask my graduate school friends about the roots. But let me for the time being concede that you all have points. Dignity does not explain immunity. Dignity is not lost in the seven exceptional situations. Dignity, unless it is the tautological equivalent of immunity, is indeed never lost when one is sued. Isn't there any other explanation for the states' immunity?"

"The national court has given a practical reason," Harvardman explained. "It's to protect the states' pocketbooks."

"I can't believe that, either," Yalewoman commented, "whether it's your concoction or the court's. States have to borrow money all the time. No one would lend to them if the states could shake off their creditors like a dog shakes off fleas. Immunity from suit and incapacity to borrow would accompany each other."

"I don't think that's quite exact as a historical matter," Simple said. "I must ask my old partner Frye how the bond market sees it. But wouldn't immunity be helpful to the states if they were sued in tort?"

"That's right, judge," said Boaltman. "Tort immunity is a valuable device and keeps state treasuries from being soaked by the plaintiffs' bar. As the court has put it, tort suits might 'threaten the financial integrity' of the states, and Congress might enact laws whose violation would lead to compensatory damages, punitive damages, and attorney fees, resulting in 'staggering burdens' on state treasuries."

"But why should the states have this shield?" Yalewoman persisted. "They're grown-up boys and girls. They're not infants. If they injure someone, why shouldn't they make the person whole? They are not more inviting targets for suit than a Microsoft. Why do they have a free ride if they trample on some lone individual? If the court fears that they will be burdened by the punitive damages, why doesn't the court hold excessive punitives a denial of due process? As for redressing an injury, elementary justice teaches that if you hurt someone you make it up to him. States should be setting an example, not getting away with murder or with toxic waste. Didn't Brandeis tell us that government is the 'omnipresent teacher'? Isn't law the omnipresent teacher? What is being taught when the highest court in the land says that it's a matter of sovereign dignity and fiscal solvency not to be liable for the mischief you have done?

"You're an ethical man, judge," Yalewoman added challengingly. "Don't you feel you're doing something unethical when you dismiss a suit against a wrongdoer simply because the wrongdoer is a sovereign? Aren't you cooperating in an injustice?"

"I've never thought of it that way," Simple replied. "If I don't have jurisdiction, I don't decide the merits of the case; I don't say that the wrongdoer is right or shouldn't redress the wrong. I simply say that I don't have the power to do anything in the case. I don't cooperate in injustice any more than any layman who lacks judicial authority. I become a bystander.

"It does seem to be sending the wrong message," Simple continued. "I don't really understand myself why the states aren't as competent to protect themselves by good lawyers and vigilant safety measures as any giant corporation. After all, even Exxon has to pay for an oil spill, and the states are better off than Exxon. They make the state laws that determine much liability, so they can arrange things to diminish their own exposure. Even federal law will be shaped by members of congress not insensitive to the protection of their home states. With all that involvement in the law on liability, I just don't know why the states need an extra dollop of security. At least I've never seen a statistical study cited by the Supreme Court to show that immunity is the sine qua non of the states' financial integrity. It's a strange figure of speech to use but the court is a bit paternalistic toward the states, as though they were still children to be coddled. It may go back to history."

"The Supreme Court has, in a way, appealed to history," Harvardman noted. "As the court once put it magisterially, 'Behind the words of the constitutional provisions are postulates which limit and control.... [Immunity] is inherent in the constitutional plan.'

"In the same vein," Harvardman went on, "a modern justice has written that immunity is a 'presupposition' of the constitution. Or, as another modern member of the court has put it, immunity is 'the background principle' that is 'embodied' in the eleventh amendment to the constitution."

"The court may have written magisterially," observed Yalewoman, "but it spoke mysteriously. What was 'the constitutional plan' not expressed in the constitution? What is a 'background principle' that does not make it to the foreground? What is a 'presupposition' that isn't put in words? I thought that the modern justices, or at least some of them, were attached to the text of the document they were expounding. If you don't have a stable text, what do you have? Anybody can guess at the background, the hidden postulates, the presuppositions of a text. It makes the constitution so open to interpretation that, as the old Southern expression goes, you could drive a team of mules through it."

"You're wrong about respect for the text of the constitution," interjected Boaltman. "The modern court has denounced fidelity to the words of the constitution as 'ahistorical literalism.'"

"Let's face it," Harvardman observed. "Law is in part a historical enterprise. The court gets nourishment from its roots. Or, to use a different metaphor, the past provides fuel for the forward motion. The real question is whether the court's history, like its logic, is screwed up."

CHAPTER 3

Votaries

That afternoon Simple found himself at the St. Wenceslas Club where he could count on seeing Fred Frye and Aeneas Ketchum of his old firm of Fish, Frye & Ketchum. "You know about the sovereign immunity of states," Simple began, "and you know that a state is immune from being sued if it wishes to be immune. Fred, you do a lot of work for brokerage houses. What does state immunity do to the state bond market?"

"Not a thing," said Frye shortly. "All munis are the same. I know, I know that the Supreme Court distinguishes cities from states, only states are immune. But not the market. A city, a county, a state agency, a state—they'll all give about the same return. If you're really worried about an issuer's credit, you'll pay for insurance. It'll cost you a little more, but you can always sue the insurer."

"You mean immunity doesn't hang over the market, telling investors that a state can revise its constitution, repudiate its bonds, and get away with it?" Simple inquired. "Suppose California had to pay some enormous energy bill and became hopelessly insolvent. Couldn't it solve its debt problem by just defaulting?"

"I suppose it could," said Frye, "and have a credit problem instead of a debt problem. The market just doesn't think that possible. As for immunity, you could count on one hand the number of bond traders who've heard of it.

"An eager young associate in our firm once brought up immunity when we were giving an opinion on a California bond issue. I told him to look at the California cases. The state had been sued a couple of times on its bonds. It had defended on various technicalities but not on grounds of immunity. State law bound the state to pay. The court opinions never mentioned immunity.

"As a matter of fact, if the solvency of the states was really behind the imposition of immunity, a state and its principal city would have to be treated as a single unit. As an investment banker recently pointed out regarding New York City: 'In the winter and spring of 1976, the State of New York was shut out of the public markets and was unable to sell its bonds because of the fiscal weakness of the city.'"

"I see," said Simple, "Supreme Court doctrine sometimes doesn't have much relevance to life. But," he went on, turning to Ketchum, "I imagine immunity is pretty important for an active state entity like the University of California."

"It is," Ketchum replied, "in my experience as outside counsel for the university. It's shielded us from an occasional tort claim and employment discrimination claim. It's also useful because we can, if we like, waive it and win a case on the merits. It works in patent cases, too. We can use it, at a bare minimum, to promote settlement."

"I imagine the idea is that the state might incur substantial losses if such an active body was subject to suit," Simple observed.

"Not a bit of it, Sam," Ketchum responded. "The United States Supreme Court held U.C. was immune when it was just acting as manager for the Atomic Energy Commission in running Livermore Lab for the federal government and any damages against U.C. would have been paid by the feds.

"Immunity, as you have learned, Sam, is a funny animal, sometimes there, sometimes gone. You might think of the doctrine as a gesture of modesty by the courts, a kind of self-denying gesture. They won't monkey in certain kinds of state business. It's true, as I've observed, that sometimes courts avoid messy tangles with a quick evocation of what they will—contrary to all sense and grammar—call the eleventh amendment. I recall that's one way a federal court got rid of a class action by Medicare recipients seeking to get a share of the state of Georgia's $4 billion recovery in the giant tobacco company settlement. Looked at from the angle of the court, I suppose, 'the eleventh amendment' was a convenient way to duck a complicated statutory exegesis.

"But from the angle of the bar and of the public, too, immunity is an invention by the Supreme Court by which it exercises its supreme power over the system. It's a doctrine so riddled with exceptions and so powerful if an exception is not allowed that the court can use it, almost at will, to produce almost any result it chooses. Sometimes it's been handy for avoiding a conflict.

Not every justice is as adroit as John Marshall in having and eating his cake. Immunity is a power-conserver for the court. Nowadays, however, immunity is being used by the court to free the states and their protean projects from federal control."

"Now that I know the university's immunity," Simple thought, "I'll drop by my old stomping ground at the Roma." Soon he was having coffee there with his graduate school friends, Cleopatra Sens, Lucinda Logic, and John Henry. "I want to get your views on the sovereign immunity of the states," he said bluntly.

"History is the key," Cleo said firmly. "At the beginning of the republic, all thirteen states were debtors and at least some of the creditors were aliens—Englishmen who had just been our enemies in war. I've read that's how John Marshall explained why the eleventh amendment was enacted. He ought to have known. He was a prominent federalist politician when the amendment was passed."

"I hope the eleventh amendment is not a diversion," Simple said. "But let's take a look at it. Here's that convenient diary provided by West Publishing Company. Will someone read the amendment aloud from the copy of the constitution printed there?"

"Here it is. I'll read it, capitals and all," said Lucinda:

The Judicial (capital J) power of the United States shall not be construed to extend to any suit in law or equity, commenced or prosecuted against one of the United States by Citizens (capital C) of another State (capital S).

"That's succinctness for you. It's amusingly modern, too—a lesson in hermeneutics. It's not the conferral of a power or the enactment of a prohibition on the exercise of governmental power. It's a rule of interpretation. It's telling someone—I suppose the judges—how they are to construe their power. I don't see that it mentions immunity."

"Of course, it doesn't," said Cleo pridefully, recalling her work in American history. "Let me tell you how the Eleventh came into existence. Robert Farquhar furnished almost ten thousand pounds sterling worth of dry goods to the state of Georgia during the American Revolution. He was not paid because middlemen kept the money. He died in 1784, leaving his claim against Georgia as part of his estate. His executor, Alexander Chisholm, a resident of Charleston, South Carolina, thought it his duty to sue to collect the debt and an additional ninety thousand pounds sterling of consequential damages. He got Edmund Randolph, a Virginian and attorney general of the United States, to represent him. In those days attorneys general supplemented their federal income with private clients, but were still called 'attorney general' as they appeared for their clients in court. Anyway, Randolph, George Washington's attorney general, brought the case before the Supreme Court. He had read article III of the constitution, whose second section reads:

> The judicial Power shall extend . . . to Controversies between two or more States;—between a State and Citizen of another State; —between Citizens of different States . . . ."

"I've been following," said Lucinda, "and I note that 'Citizen' is capitalized as well as 'State,' putting 'Citizen' and 'State' on an orthographic par."

"I'm not quite through reading," said Cleo. "Section 2 of article III goes on to say:

In all Cases . . . in which a State shall be Party, the Supreme
Court shall have original Jurisdiction.

The whole of paragraph 1, as you see, deals with what we now
call 'diversity jurisdiction'; that is, it deals with cases where the
plaintiffs and defendants come from different states. The First
Congress, a number of whose members had helped to draft or to
ratify the constitution, followed up on article III by passing a
statute in 1789. It read:

> The supreme court shall have exclusive jurisdiction of all
> controversies where a state is a party, except between a state
> and its citizens; and except also, between a state and citizens
> of other states and aliens, in which latter case it shall have
> original but not exclusive jurisdiction.

Congress didn't use any capitals, not even for the court. You will
note that the statute, like article III itself, is drafted with some
care, a lawyer's care. It uses the word 'between' for cases involving states and out-of-state citizens; it doesn't say 'where states
are plaintiffs' or anything like that. You will also note the lawyer-
ly caution in saying that jurisdiction is not being granted in a
case between a state and one of its own citizens. I say it was done
with caution because article III itself didn't provide jurisdiction
in such a case, but apparently the First Congress thought it wise
to be explicit. They couldn't have believed that the sovereign
immunity of the states would do the trick. In that way the first
congressmen were not like our modern justices for whom sovereign immunity is central.

"But I'm getting away from the story. Randolph had read article III and the judiciary act of 1789 and he knew he could bring

Chisholm's case against Georgia in the Supreme Court. Georgia
didn't agree. It refused to make an appearance. That legal ma-
neuver didn't keep it from submitting a stiff 'remonstrance and
protestation' written by two top attorneys, Charles Ingersoll and
Alexander Dallas, that gave the five justices (the whole court in
those days) something to chew on.

"The majority agreed with Randolph. I won't attempt to repeat all they said, for they spoke seriatim, and each had something to say, and they didn't spare repetition. The first to speak,
Justice James Iredell, was a minority of one, not believing in sovereign immunity on constitutional grounds but asserting that
Congress had not legislated on the subject before the court. At
common law, an individual could not sue the sovereign. As there
was neither federal nor common law authorizing the suit, the
case should be dismissed. Iredell had heard the case originally
sitting on circuit in Augusta, so he had a sense of the intense local feeling. He now took note of Randolph's remark 'let me hope
and pray, that not a single star in the American constellation will
ever suffer its lustre to be diminished, by hostility against the
sentence of a court, which itself has adopted.' Iredell prayed to
God that if his views were not adopted, none of the evils with
which the case was pregnant would ensue.

"Two of the majority were quite succinct. Justice John Blair,
a signer of the constitution, said, 'A dispute between A and B is
surely a dispute between B and A.' The court had jurisdiction.
Justice William Cushing noted the argument that to take jurisdiction would 'reduce states to mere corporations and take away
all sovereignty.' He observed that there were many abridgments
of state sovereignty effected by the constitution. Where sovereignty was abridged it was for the good of the whole.

"Justice James Wilson, another signer of the constitution, was magnificent. He began with a fundamental observation: 'To the constitution of the United States the term *sovereign* is totally unknown.' He went on to say that a state was a wonderful contrivance but that it was man-made, not divine, and it acted by human beings. Was there a reason 'that a state, any more than the men who compose it, ought not to do justice and fulfill engagements? It will not be pretended that there is....' A dishonest state, like a dishonest merchant, was amenable to a court of justice. What was the point of the constitution providing in so many words in article I that a state may not 'pass any law impairing the obligations of contracts,' if the state was not subject to a 'controlling judiciary power'? The people of the United States had formed the Union 'to establish justice.' Accepting that purpose when it entered the Union, Georgia had submitted to the jurisdiction of the federal judiciary.

"Chief Justice John Jay, co-author of *The Federalist*, declared that sovereignty had passed from the king of Great Britain to the people of the United States, and the people had established the constitution, leaving a residual sovereignty in the people of each state. Sovereignty in the American sense was not like the sovereignty of a European prince. Here there were no subjects. Here there were no inferiors. Any citizen could sue another citizen or forty thousand citizens, as would be the case if a citizen sued the city of Philadelphia. Could a citizen not in the same way sue the fifty thousand citizens of Delaware 'associated under a state government'? What made a state government superior to a city or a citizen? Any difference would not correspond with the equal rights we claim or the equality we profess. Moreover, the United States had taken a place among the nations of the earth and was bound by the law of nations. It was fitting that the United States establish justice by providing that a case against a state by citizens of another state not be judged by the courts of the defendant state but by an impartial national tribunal. Four to one, the justices ordered Georgia to respond to the suit.

"I must admit," added Cleo, "that I wrote my thesis on the case and have been quoting liberally from it. I thought one got pretty close to knowing 'original intent' when I read the words of two signers and a contributor to *The Federalist*. The case itself, if you're interested, fizzled out. Georgia settled."

"We didn't think you knew *Chisholm* by heart," John Henry commented. "What's most striking about your recitation is how those old justices were concerned about establishing justice and not letting the states be immune if they impaired a contract. I wonder why our modern justices don't have comparable sensitivity."

"It seems to me that all five justices, plus Washington's attorney general, plus the members of the First Congress, didn't have the idea of the modern justices that sovereign immunity was somehow built into the constitution," Cleo added. "But I haven't quite finished. *Chisholm* was not a popular decision. Congress at once proposed the eleventh amendment, which as you have noted tells the judges how to construe part of article III, so the constitution is now contrary to *Chisholm*. The states were let off the hook as far as out-of-state creditors suing in diversity went."

"What does it all show as to the states' immunity?" asked Simple.

"Almost nothing, except that there were different views as to what was desirable. The eleventh amendment took away federal jurisdiction in one class of cases without saying a word on immunity. Then John Marshall got into the act," Cleo concluded.

"We all know about Chief Justice Marshall from history and from Con Law," John Henry interjected. "In *Marbury v. Madison* he established the Supreme Court's power of reviewing federal legislation. He was a devoted federalist and he extended federal power. He wasn't about to let the eleventh amendment or anything like sovereign immunity block the expansion of federal power over the states. He invented two major paths for end runs around such obstacles."

"What were the two paths?" inquired Simple.

"Marshall cut one road using the same technique he had in *Marbury v. Madison,*" John Henry responded. "That is, he announced a bold principle but did not let it affect the end result, so the principle was established but the party against whom it was established could not effectively oppose it because the principle was not applied to that party's detriment. It's a pretty good way of having your cake and eating it.

"In modern jargon some call it 'the passive-aggressive approach,' he added, "but I'd call it the aggressive-passive approach —assert your principle and hold back enforcement of it. As Marshall himself put it, he was 'not fond of butting against a wall in sport.' So he stated the principle and left its enforcement to the future."

"What was the principle?" Simple asked a bit impatiently.

"Let me set out the facts first," John Henry pleaded. "Philip Cohen and Mendes Cohen, two brothers, were convicted in the borough court of Norfolk, Virginia, of selling six lottery tickets contrary to Virginia law and were fined $100, a substantial sum of money. There was no state court to hear an appeal from the borough court, so their appeal went directly to the Supreme Court of the United States as they had raised a federal defense. The defense was that the lottery tickets were issued by the city of Washington as part of the Grand National Lottery, whose proceeds went to finance the capital. The case was styled *Cohens v. Virginia*, a curious mushing together of the two defendants as though they were a single entity, a touch of anti-semitism perhaps. Virginia moved to dismiss the case on the ground that, as a sovereign, Virginia was free to punish violations of its laws. Two weeks later, Marshall, writing for a unanimous court, denied Virginia's motion.

"Here we come to the principle. Marshall distinguished the two parts of article III of the constitution. One part created jurisdiction over cases depending on the parties. That had been the part involved in *Chisholm*. The other part gave jurisdiction 'over all Cases, in Law and Equity, arising under this Constitution, the laws of the United States, and treaties made, or which shall be made, under their Authority.' Construing this section, Marshall wrote, 'This clause extends the jurisdiction of the Court to all the cases described, without making in its terms any exceptions whatever, and without any regard to the condition of the party.' A state could not be sued without its consent, Marshall said he would not deny; but the consent did not have to be given each time in every case. The states had given their consent to the constitution. That consent included consent to the grant of jurisdiction in article III. The 'spirit of the constitution' was not contrary to this conclusion. Accordingly, 'whoever may be the parties,' the court had jurisdiction when the case arose out of the laws of the United States. The eleventh amendment had no application. Moreover, the amendment had no bearing on a defendant's appeal from a state court to the Supreme Court, nor did it apply at all when, as here, the suit did not involve out-of-state citizens.

"You can note the strength of Marshall's demonstration," John Henry gratuitously added. "The constitution in this part of article III speaks of 'all Cases.' Marshall takes it that 'all' means 'all.'

"Albert Beveridge, Marshall's most politically astute biographer, calls *Cohens* a 'remarkable state paper,' an 'address,' delivered at the time of the national crisis over the admission of Missouri to the Union, on the supremacy of the Union over 'the sections.'"

"How did he insulate his holding from objection?" asked Simple, desirous to know the trick.

"After he had announced his opinion denying Virginia's motion to dismiss, the merits of the case were then argued, Daniel Webster appearing by appointment of the court for Virginia. The court held that Congress had merely authorized the sale of lottery tickets but had not provided for their sale outside the district. The brothers' defense failed. The judgment of the borough court was affirmed."

"What was the other path around the eleventh amendment?" asked Simple.

"The officer's suit, the path the Supreme Court later took in *Ex parte Young,*" John Henry responded. "It was actually an old English device for letting a case go forward against the crown without bringing in the king as a defendant. Marshall made it an American vehicle in *Osborn v. Bank of the United States.* Marshall had already held in *McCullough v. Maryland* in 1819 that it was unconstitutional for a state to tax the nationally chartered bank, and he had asserted federal jurisdiction over the state when it sought to collect the unconstitutional tax. At the very time *Mc-Cullough* was being argued in 1819, Ohio imposed a tax of $50,000 a day on each office of any bank in the state that had not been chartered by the state, exhibiting, as it were, Marshall's dictum that the power to tax is the power to destroy. Ralph Osborn, the state auditor, sent three agents to Chillicothe, Ohio, to extract $100,000 from an office of the Bank of the United States in operation there. The bank had already secured a federal injunction against Osborn, and the agents collected the $100,000 in violation of the injunction. The cash was delivered to the state treasurer, who kept it in a separate account, less $2,000 paid the state collectors as a fee. In federal court the bank sued Osborn for recovery of the $100,000. The real party in interest was the state. Osborn no longer had the cash; the bank couldn't have secured it from him. Marshall, without dissent, upheld the power of the court to compel restitution. 'The party named in the record' was not the state. In short, a suit against the state's officer was not a suit against the state, even when the state would end up paying the judgment."

"I'm indebted to you both," said Simple, turning to Cleo and John Henry, "for your exposition of the law as it was understood by the Jay and Marshall courts. Need anything more be said?"

"I think it's interesting how little immunity stood in the way at a time when the states were relatively powerful in relation to the federal government," observed Cleo. "The federal government did not have its own police force. Federal courts lacked troops to enforce their judgments. Despite carping states-righters, Marshall carried the day. There are a few more cases of the Marshall court worth noting for the ease with which states were subjected to federal power. I'm thinking of *Martin v. Hunter's Lessee* where the Supreme Court of Virginia took the position that a civil judgment by that court was not subject to review in the United States Supreme Court, advancing the theory that the constitution did not authorize federal action upon a sovereign state. Writing for a unanimous court (Marshall having recused himself), Justice Joseph Story stated: 'It is a mistake, that the constitution was not designed to operate upon states, in their corporate capacities. It is crowded with provisions which restrain or annul the sovereignty of states in some of the highest branches of their prerogatives. The tenth section of the first article contains a long list of disabilities and prohibitions upon the states. Surely, when such essential portions of state sovereignty are taken away, or prohibited to be exercised, it cannot be correctly asserted that the constitution does not act upon the states.' Those words appear to be forgotten by today's court.

"Then there's *Worcester v. Georgia* where Samuel A. Worcester, a Congregational minister authorized by the president of the United States to carry out missionary activity in the Cherokee Territory, was convicted in the superior court of Gwinett County, Georgia, of entering the Indian territory without a state license and sentenced to four years of hard labor. His appeal from the judgment—not a habeas action against a Georgia warden—went directly to the Supreme Court of the United States. Relying on his reasoning in *Cohens* without bothering to repeat it, Marshall took jurisdiction, found federal law violated by the state's prosecution, and ordered the prisoner freed."

"I take it that these two cases illustrate one exception I've already noticed in modern law," Simple observed dryly, "as to Supreme Court jurisdiction over the states when the case is appealed. Do we need to know more about the history of this tattered immunity doctrine?"

"We have to face *Hans*," John Henry said gloomily.

"Tell us about *Hans*," Simple suggested.

"It's the climax in 1890 of a series of cases in which the Supreme Court declined to enforce bonds which had been issued by the state of Louisiana and had been guaranteed to be paid by its constitution," reported John Henry. "Every device the bondholders tried was faulted by the court. A suit against the state's financial officers was said to force the court to assume 'the administration of the fiscal affairs of the state.' Bondholders then assigned their bonds to the states of New Hampshire and New York, who then brought suit against Louisiana. Article III provided for states to sue each other; the eleventh amendment was apparently no bar. The Supreme Court treated the two Northern states as the agents of out-of-state plaintiffs; the eleventh amendment became a bar. Finally, Bernard Hans, a citizen of Louisiana, sued the state on the bonds. The Louisiana constitution, by amendment in 1874, had designated the consolidated bonds issued in that year 'a valid obligation of the state' and provided that, to secure their payment, 'the judicial power shall be exercised when necessary.' The Louisiana constitution of 1880 had superseded the 1874 constitution, and Louisiana had diverted to its general expenses the taxes meant to pay the bonds. The state had, therefore, sought to impair the validity of its contract with the bondholders in violation of article I, section 10 of the constitution of the United States. As Hans was a citizen of the state, the eleventh amendment was no bar. His case arose under the laws of the United States and so, under the judiciary act of 1875, was cognizable in federal court.

"Writing for the Supreme Court, Justice Joseph Bradley found Hans's suit 'anomalous and unheard of when the constitution was adopted.' If it had any basis, it was by appealing to 'the letter,' not the spirit, of the constitution. What the constitution meant was decided by the voice of eminent authorities interpreting it while its ratification was being considered, authorities quoted in the brief for Louisiana. In Number 81 of *The Federalist*, Alexander Hamilton had answered opponents of the proposed constitution, who feared that the assignment of state bonds to out-of-state citizens would permit them to sue the state under article III. Hamilton declared this fear to be without foundation: 'It is inherent in the nature of sovereignty not to be amenable to the suit of an individual without its consent. This is the general sense and the general practice of mankind; and the exemption, as one of the attributes of sovereignty, is now enjoyed by the government of every state in the Union.'

"In the Virginia ratifying convention, James Madison had also met objection to the clause creating federal jurisdiction over a controversy between a state and citizens of another state. He explained the clause as applying only to a case where a state was the plaintiff. 'It is not,' he said, 'in the power of individuals to call any state into court.' John Marshall, another delegate to the convention, met the same objection in precisely the same way, adding, 'It is not rational to suppose that the sovereign power should be dragged before a court.'

"As chief justice, Marshall adopted a different line in *Cohens*, Bradley conceded, but what Marshall wrote there was not necessary to decide the case and so could be dismissed as 'extrajudicial,' not binding precedent. The eleventh amendment did not assert a state's sovereign immunity from suit by its own citizens because the suability of a state without consent was 'a thing unknown to the law.'

"Bradley rounded out his opinion by declaring *Chisholm v. Georgia* to have been wrongly decided. Georgia had been immune from suit. Indeed, on Bradley's analysis, the eleventh amendment had been unnecessary; the court could have corrected its own mistake."

"How odd," Lucinda remarked, "that *Hans* has sometimes been read, even by the Supreme Court, as if it enlarged the eleventh amendment. In fact, *Hans* makes the eleventh amendment superfluous.

"Sometimes it seems as if the court used 'the eleventh amendment' as shorthand for state sovereign immunity. But what this usage really does is to give the court a rhetorical boost. The court seems to be citing the constitution when all the court actually has to conjure with is its own judicially created immunity for the states."

"What law did give immunity to Louisiana in *Hans*?" Simple inquired.

"Justice Bradley doesn't say," replied John Henry. "It wasn't natural law, although a modern dissenter speculated that natural law was what lay behind *Hans* immunity. Natural law, at least as conceived by Aristotle and Aquinas, doesn't pretend to determine the powers of a state. Bradley says if you want to know the reason for sovereign immunity, read 'the writers on public law.' The authorities he invokes seem to rely on custom or on common law or the law of nations.

"Of course, the law of nations would not be relevant unless the states, just brought back into the Union by force, were thought of as independent nations. Custom is scarcely different from common law. The common law was the common law of England, keeping the monarch from being personally cited to appear in court. You would think common law could be overcome by the constitution plus a federal statute. Somehow making common law sovereignty a presupposition of the eleventh amendment, Bradley gave common law immunity a kind of constitutional gloss."

"Why are we interested in *Hans*?" Simple persisted. "Aren't the recent decisions of the Supreme Court enough?"

"Of course, they are, judge," said John Henry. "But *Hans* is an icon of the modern court. *Hans* repudiated John Marshall's federal question approach to jurisdiction. It made state immunity central. It brought into the discourse of the Supreme Court the opinions on immunity of Hamilton, Madison, and the young Marshall. The modern court needs *Hans* as a reference point, a precedent, a reassurance. Even more, the court needs those three great names to conjure with."

"History is a powerful force," Cleo murmured with some self-satisfaction. "If you grasp its direction, it will carry you with it. Then there are those who try to hitch a lift with history but whose destination is not where history is going. The Supreme Court seems to me like such a hitchhiker."

"You two have talked a lot about history, but I'd start by examining what a state is as a matter of semantics," Lucinda broke in. "You see, 'state' is one of those entities like 'corporation.' It's a legal term. In the nineteenth century it was debated whether such entities were real or fictional, and points were made on both sides. Of course, a state was real—it could hurt you. Of course, it wasn't real—it was people arranged in a certain order. We see now that it has a reality in terms of a system. It's just like 'strike' or 'out' in baseball. They are terms that have meaning and reality but only within the rules of baseball. They are neither metaphysical realities nor fiction. So, in our legal system, a 'state' has the meaning and reality assigned to it by the system. There's nothing inherent in the term. It has the meaning the system chooses to give it. Now if the system assigns immunity as an attribute to the legal arrangement the system calls the state, it's perfectly doable. But immunity doesn't come as a necessary accompaniment of being a state. What counts as a state and what counts as its characteristics depend on choices made in the system."

"Your approach reminds me a little of Justice James Wilson's in *Chisholm*," Simple said. "The state is man-made. I assume that means we can make of it what is convenient and just."

"A striking assumption of the supporters of state sovereignty," Lucinda observed, "is that all of the fifty states were once sovereigns by themselves, so that they could enter the Union with their 'sovereignty intact,' as the Supreme Court has thrice put it. True, the original thirteen and Texas were once such independent sovereigns. The other thirty-six either were territories of the United States or were carved out of existing states without ever having had an independent existence. The majority of states, thus, were never sovereigns; but the court has observed that each was admitted to the Union on an "equal footing" with the original, thereby acquiring their sovereign rights by the act of admission.

"That it has not proved difficult to fit the new states in with the old is a sign, and confirmation, of the fact that the original thirteen were never treated by the federal constitution as sovereigns. The states created by fiat of Congress stand on equal footing with the original thirteen, because all the states that are are subordinate parts of a nation whose supreme law is supplied by the constitution and by Congress. The legal system, without difficulty, assigns each state the same characteristics."

"The state also has a kind of theological overhang," chimed in Cleo. "The overhang somehow affects our imagination. You knew the first great English celebration of the state as such was Thomas Hobbes's *Leviathan* where the sovereign has the power to coin money; to dispose of the estates and persons of infants; to have preemption in the markets; to control the militia; to control all doctrines; and to decide all controversies which may arise concerning law, either civil or natural. These powers, Hobbes says, cannot be communicated to others or be separated from each other. The authority of the sovereign is 'indivisible,' because without that indivisible authority, contention will break out and society resolve itself into a state of nature. Such an imagined sovereign can never injure any subject, for the subjects have ceded to him to do whatever he sees fit to do; they have no rights against such a ruler. The sovereign cannot be subject to law, for that subjection would set a sovereign above the sovereign.

"The Hobbesian state is a substitute for God. Now, for John Calvin, in particular, power was the capital characteristic of a God to whom all honor was due. So, if the state was to be a kind of secular substitute for God, power with honor was essential for it.

"Joseph Bradley, who wrote *Hans*, was a liberal Christian— hence his emphasis on spirit as opposed to letter—but he'd been brought up a Calvinist in the Dutch Reformed Church. Is it implausible that echoes of Calvin on the majesty of God can be found in Bradley's devotion to the sovereign?

"Take Holmes, for another example," she continued. "He was fierce in asserting the prerogatives of the sovereign—for example, in the *American Banana* case letting Costa Rica as a sovereign be the shield of the United Fruit Company, even though, if you looked beneath the surface, United Fruit owned Costa Rica. In Holmes's view, 'repeatedly voiced, the authority that makes the law is itself superior to it'—the same view that a voluntarist theologian such as Duns Scotus had of God. God could not be bound by any law; what God willed was right. Since the state, like the deity, is superior to the law, one cannot sue the sovereign, Holmes says, on 'the logical and practical ground that there can be no legal right as against the authority that makes the law on which the right depends.'"

"Logical and practical ground?" Lucinda queried. "In the United States there is no single unitary authority. Congress can make laws that bind the government of the United States. Congress can even bind itself. There is no logical difficulty, and there is no practical difficulty, in one branch of government enforcing laws made by another branch. What is Holmes echoing except Calvin's notion of God, a sovereign who is not bound by any law because He creates the law, a sovereign who can't be sued or complained about? Holmes, I believe, was the first avowed atheist to sit on the Supreme Court. He managed to transmute his theological heritage into a concept of the sovereign state."

"Well," Simple mused, "I hear the theological echoes, although they're pretty remote. Since you're into history, I'd like to get Cleo's take on *Hans*."

"*Hans* was an extraordinary break, not only with John Marshall but with fairly recent decisions of the court that decided *Hans*," Cleo responded. "Morever, it was a court dominated by

Northerners and Republicans. Joseph Bradley himself had been appointed by President Grant. It was a pro-capitalist court. What was it doing giving a break to an old Confederate state, letting newly returned Democrats destroy the state constitution enacted by Republicans and at the same time running a risk of roiling the bond market? Taken at face value, and not confined to its facts, *Hans* jeopardized the creditworthiness of every state in the Union. They all became potential deadbeats that could prevent themselves from being sued on their bonds anytime they chose to change their statutes or their constitutions. I recite these interesting facts in order to suggest that there must have been some overriding objective that Bradley and company were trying to achieve."

"What could that have been?" asked Simple.

"Reconciliation with the South, or at least nonconfrontation with the South. Remember, federal troops had substantially been withdrawn from the South after the election of 1876. The country was tired of reconstruction. The African Americans were being abandoned. Northern capital was more interested in ending the conflict than in aiding the ex-slaves. If push had come to shove with the Louisiana legislature, the Supreme Court didn't have the troops to compel it to obey. So, the justices must have thought, it was the path of prudence to abandon precedent rather than have rebellion and rejection."

"That kind of historical explanation for the doctrinal move in *Hans* has been objected to, objected to strongly by the court itself," John Henry interposed.

"It's all a matter of inference," Cleo replied sweetly. "But if you see a boulder falling down a mountain, you can infer that the earth has moved or someone has pushed it, and then you can investigate and eliminate one of the causes. I don't see any internal cause here, and the boulder did roll."

"What about the voices of the three great advocates of the constitution?" John Henry rejoined. "It was a century earlier, but maybe for that very reason their words were cloaked with authority. They were the founding fathers. It's not unknown in the history of doctrine for great truths to be rescued from obscurity. It could be that's what Hans's attorneys did for Hamilton, Madison, and Marshall."

"If so," Cleo replied sharply, "they were heard out of context. To begin with, they were, at the time they wrote or spoke, trying to get the constitution adopted. I won't say they lied, but they certainly put the best possible construction on its clauses. Second, they all responded to objections aimed at the diversity clause, the one that spoke of the states as parties. There was no reason for any of them taking on the extra burden of explaining or defending federal question jurisdiction. As to what they thought on that, Madison referred explicitly in *The Federalist* to 'the trial of controversies in which the States may be parties,' noted that there would be controversies relating to 'the boundaries' of national and state power, and observed that these controversies would be settled by the tribunal 'established under the general government.' In the same essay, Madison spoke of the sovereignty of the states as 'residuary and inviolable.' Plainly their sovereignty was only inviolable in its residual aspect; it was not intact and inviolable. Madison also made manifest that '[u]ltimate authority resides in the people alone,' that is, that the people are the only complete sovereign. Madison also thought that the federal government would have few agents and that it would federalize the state courts as part of the judicial system, so the sovereign states could have been yoked into federal teams.

Marshall made his thought perfectly plain in *Cohens*: Federal question jurisdiction existed, 'whoever were the parties.' As for Hamilton, he had expressed himself in *The Federalist* Number 80 by tracking the words of article III as to each kind of jurisdiction that article granted and by defending not only federal question jurisdiction but diversity jurisdiction over a controversy between one state and citizens of another as 'perhaps not less essential to the peace of the Union than that which has just been examined.' Granted that he backed up on this point in Number 81, he still didn't limit the sweep of federal question jurisdiction, because he indicated that the states had ceded their sovereignty where the federal constitution granted power to the nation. As he put it tactfully but firmly in Number 81 itself, the states had immunity '[u]nless, therefore, there is a surrender of this immunity in the plan of the constitution.' The reference to 'the plan of the constitution' is an unmistakable reference to Number 80 where he lists 'the proper objects' of the federal judiciary and observes that 'the plan of the constitution' prohibits the states from doing certain things. Undoubtedly, Hamilton thought that the federal judiciary could prevent or restrain actions of the states in violation of article I.

"'The truth is,' Cleo quoted, 'that difficulties on this point are inherent in the nature of the Federal Constitution; they result inevitably from a division of the legislative power.' That's the neutral-sounding observation of Hamilton. But Hamilton wasn't neutral on how such difficulties should be resolved. He made that observation in the course of advising President Washington on the constitutionality of creating a national bank. Not a word in the constitution spoke of Congress having the power to create a bank. Congressional power, Hamilton thought, was not confined to 'the literal meaning': an 'adherence to the letter of its powers would at once arrest the motions of government.' The criterion of the constitutional was 'the *end* to which the measure relates as *means*.' The power to achieve the end implied the power to use the means adapted to that end. Congress had power to collect taxes, to borrow money, to regulate interstate commerce, and to maintain fleets and armies. A national bank was proper means to each of these ends, and it was a means that was necessary in the broad sense of being useful in serving these ends. Accepting Hamilton's advice and rejecting that of Jefferson, Washington signed the bill creating the Bank of the United States.

"The basic controversy continued to boil within the cabinet," Cleo added. "Jefferson maintained that Hamilton's policies had led to a 'corrupt squadron,' determined 'to get rid of the limitations imposed by the constitution on the general legislature, limitations on the faith of which the states acceded to the constitution.' Hamilton wrote Washington putting the question, 'How shall it be determined which side is right?' He then answered the question:

There are some things which the General Government has clearly a right to do—there are others which it has clearly no right to meddle with, and there is a good deal of middle ground, about which honest & well disposed men may differ. The most that can be said is that some of this middle ground may have been occupied by the National Legislature; and this surely is no evidence of a disposition to get

rid of the limitations in the constitution; nor can it be
viewed in that light by men of candor.

The middle ground was what Hamilton claimed for Congress. As to 'the Antifederal Champions' there was one convincing answer: 'That the beneficial effects of the Government have
exceeded expectation and are witnessed by the general prosper-
ity of the Nation.'"

"Immunity of the states," Simple remarked, "does not seem
to be the subject of this debate."

"The principle of immunity was," Cleo interjected. "If the
national legislature has the implied power to achieve the ends
the constitution has assigned it, it has the power to make the
states conform. It's the national legislature's prerogative to occupy the middle ground of sovereignty.

Alexander Hamilton was the foremost Federalist of all in his
championing of federal power over the states. He was openly
contemptuous of the confederacy that had been the governmental system that the constitution was replacing. He was contemptuous of the supporters of that system— 'credulous votaries of
state power,' he called them in *The Federalist* Number 60. It is
the very height of irony that Hamilton should be evoked by the
modern Supreme Court to limit federal jurisdiction over the
states. It is also profoundly ahistorical."

"I bow to your exposition of the history," John Henry said
graciously. "I do believe that the development of doctrine takes
some odd turns. Context is fundamental. Hamilton, Madison,
and Marshall just can't be lifted out of context, packaged in
a brief, and quoted by today's Supreme Court. You have made
these defenders of the constitution coherent with themselves."

"As a matter of fact," Cleo added a bit archly, "there is a constitution that Joseph Bradley and his companions in *Hans* might have heard of, and that they might have been expounding. It's the constitution of the Confederate States of America, adopted March 11, 1861. The preamble identifies the parties as 'We, the people of the Confederate States, each State acting in its sovereign and independent character.' The sovereignty of the states is not in the background; it's front and center. Article III, section 2 of the Confederate constitution setting out the judicial power provides for its extension to suits 'between a State and citizens of another State, where the State is plaintiff.' No ambiguity there, either."

"Touché," John Henry jocularly cried. "*Hans* and the modern cases seem less a development of doctrine than a corruption of doctrine—always a possibility as I know Newman maintained. As he put it, a doctrine, to be a true development, must have vigor and a vital connection with its origins. Frankly, speaking now as a nonspecialist in this area, I don't see the vital connection of immunity with the constitution as understood by its framers and its great expounder, Marshall. Nor, to tell the truth, do I see the vigor. Immunity is pretty close to sterility. The courts are sterilized as sources of justice. Where is the passion of a Wilson or a Jay that a constitution created to establish justice must assure that the courts provide justice?"

"Let me see if I can sum up what I now know," said Simple. "Immunity is a common law doctrine. It was probably believed to be in force by Marshall, Madison, and Hamilton. But Marshall held that the immunity was waived by the states as to federal questions when the states ratified the constitution. Hamilton was almost as clear. Madison did not address waiver.

There's nothing to support the view that immunity was part of the constitutional design or inherent in its plan.

"Immunity works only because of the seven exceptions to it. The most important of these, the suit against an officer, works only because its self-contradiction is happily ignored. Of the reasons supporting the doctrine, one is a tautology, the other is utterly unusable by a modern state that wants to keep its credit. The chief practical effect is to shield not only state government but many subsidiary state agencies from complying with federal laws enacted for the good of all."

"The invention of immunity—is it the addition of an important tool for the Supreme Court to use in its discretion as it shapes our system? Or have we become 'credulous votaries of state power'?" Simple asked himself as he headed home. The cases now to be reviewed provide an answer, not free from ambiguity, to Simple's question.

CHAPTER 4

The Sovereign Publisher and the Last of the Menu Girls

THE UNBEARABLE DISPROPORTIONATENESS OF PATENT PROTECTION

Peter Roberts had an inspiration, or so it seemed to him. Everyone he knew was complaining about college tuition. It was rising every year everywhere. How could parents be sure they had put enough aside to assure their children a college education when the time came? Suddenly Roberts had the answer: Devise a scheme that would be devoted to saving parents' money for college. Guarantee that when the time came there would be enough to pay for the education the parents wanted for their child.

How was this feat to be accomplished? First, the cost of college, say, ten years from now, would have to be calculated, projecting the current rate of inflation and the especially high average annual rise in college tuition. Then determine what sum invested today at an assumed rate of interest would equal this amount. With these calculations made, a financial product could be sold as a way of providing the college education desired. In 1984, Roberts designed a computer program to make the necessary calculations, spelled them out in fifty-six pages of technical detail, and applied for a patent on the algorithms he employed.

A process is patentable. A principle is not. The Supreme Court has drawn a line between patentable and unpatentable computer algorithms that is so fine that a leading commentator on patents declares that the difference can be understood and applied on only "the most excruciating case-by-case basis." Arguably, at least, the algorithms of Roberts were eligible for patentability. The patent statute required that they also be useful and new; a "new use" met both requirements.

Undeniably, the program was useful. Was it new? While Robert's application was still pending before the United States Patent Office in 1986, the University of Michigan began to offer a prepaid college plan. Parents could pay now what the university estimated the tuition would be x years from now. The university, trusting that it could invest the parents' money well, guaranteed that their child would not be charged more when x years had elapsed and the child was ready for admission. Roberts's scheme was similar except that he could not guarantee what a given college would charge in x years, and he had to depend on his investment skills, not on the resources of a large university, to make enough in the intervening years to stay in business.

Doubts set aside, Roberts called his patent "Methods and Apparatus for Funding Future Liability of Uncertain Cost." On January 26, 1988, the United States Patent Office issued to him U.S. Patent No. 4,722,055. Roberts transferred the patent to a new bank he had founded, appropriately named College Savings Bank. The bank called its principal product the CollegeSure certificate of deposit.

In 1989, a year after the patent was issued and three years after Michigan's example, the Florida Prepaid Postsecondary Education Expense Board offered to all Florida residents a prepaid college plan on the Michigan model. The legislature created the board and provided for its funding by a mix of appropriated funds and the deposits it received from parents. The actual providers were to be banks and insurance companies. The statute further authorized a "marketing" entity, which would not only sell the programs but choose a "trustee service firm" to select and supervise the investments. The statute thoughtfully provided that neither the state nor the board could be held liable for misrepresentation by the marketing entity.

As the plan was marketed, it was divided into three programs: one to cover tuition, one to cover health and student activity fees, one to cover dormitory costs. The programs were meant to meet these needs at Florida's eleven state universities and twenty-eight community colleges, all with corporate charters distinct from the general government of the state, with the community colleges having a local character that further distanced them from the general government. Far from exclusively funding statewide activity, the marketing aspect of the plan was emphasized by a provision that beneficiaries could use the money at any qualified private university in or out of the state. The board solicited business, asking, "Will you be ready for college when your kids are?" In sum, the Florida plan was a state-sponsored enterprise intermixed with a considerable amount of commercial activity and designed to attract not only users of the state system of higher education but patrons of private colleges. By 1995, the Education Expense Board had sold about 270,000 plans and had assets of over $1 billion.

Meanwhile, Roberts's College Savings Bank (CSB) had had success, but on a more modest scale. It had sold 10,000 plans and had $80 million in assets. It looked with envy at Florida and at fifteen other states which were essentially its competitors in the prepaid state college market. Roberts decided the time had come to assert his patented method for providing a definite amount of money by a definite date in the future. College Savings Bank sued the Education Expense Board.

CSB indeed filed two suits, one charging the Education Expense Board with patent infringement, the other charging it with falsely advertising its product, a tort under the federal Lanham Act. Organized as a bank in Princeton, New Jersey, CSB chose as its forum the federal district court in Trenton. The course of the two suits then diverged, determined by the difference between the two claims.

Article I of the constitution of the United States provides:

> The Congress shall have Power ... to promote the Progress of Science and useful Arts, by securing for limited Times to Authors and Inventors the exclusive Right to their respective Writings and Discoveries.

The patent and copyright powers of Congress are among the powers explicitly enumerated by the constitution, like the powers to levy taxes, raise an army, or issue currency. The enumerated powers are what the framers of the constitution saw as fundamental to the new federal government.

The First Congress made it its business to pass a bill authorizing the issuance of patents and providing for their protection. On April 15, 1790, President Washington signed the bill into law. "[E]very person" who violated a patent was made liable in damages. No exception for the states was written into the first patent law or into later amendments. On occasion a state or a state agency was alleged to be an infringer and was sued in a federal court, where plaintiffs were met by a defense of state immunity. Only as the protection of property under section 5 of the fourteenth amendment could protection of a patent be asserted against a state. Then in 1985, the Supreme Court stated that when Congress exercised section 5 power under the fourteenth amendment, its intent to override state immunity must be made explicit. In 1990, the Federal Circuit applied this teaching of the Supreme Court, found no explicit abrogation of immunity in the patent law, and consequently held a state department of transportation immune from suit as an infringer. This precedent might have seemed to block CSB's suit.

Two years later, however, Congress had apparently obviated the difficulty by enacting the Patent and Plant Variety Protection Remedy Clarification Act of 1992. Its statutory purpose was "to clarify" that the states were subject to suit by any person for infringement and subject to all the remedies "that can be obtained in a suit against a private person." The statute defined what it meant by "whoever infringes": "whoever includes any State, any instrumentality of a State, and any officer or employee of a State." As if that were not enough, the statute specified, "Any

State, any instrumentality of a State and any officer or employee of a State...shall not be immune, under the eleventh amendment...or under any other doctrine of sovereign immunity...."

Obeying the statute, the district court refused to grant immunity against the Roberts patent claim. The Federal Circuit, to which all patent appeals go, affirmed. The Federal Circuit reasoned that a patent was property; that under the fourteenth amendment Congress could prevent a state from arbitrarily invading this property; and that Congress had indisputably removed all immunity. Applying the *Boerne* test of proportionality, the circuit found the remedy proportionate. The law did not restrain the state in any of its core functions. The law merely put state enterprises on a par with others in the commercial world of patents. That there were evils to be remedied or prevented was clear from the patent suits that had been brought against the states. The substantial increase of activity in research by state universities, especially in biotechnology, pointed in the same direction. The universities were active in a field where patents played a significant part.

The Education Expense Board obtained certiorari from the Supreme Court, and its prospects brightened as it marshaled the current court's teaching on the immunity of sovereigns (the board's status as arm of the sovereign being unchallenged), the need for a legislative record establishing an evil, and the requirement of a proportionate legislative response. The solicitor general of the United States joined CSB in arguing that the patent statute trumped the claimed immunity.

The Supreme Court chose the occasion to show that the criteria set out in *Boerne* were not a one-time answer to RFRA but rather constitutional law by which all of Congress's legislation under the fourteenth amendment would be judged. The four dissenters themselves did not challenge the criteria, only their application. For the majority, Congress had flunked the *Boerne* tests.

To begin with, no evil to be remedied or prevented had been established in evidence before Congress. The House Report noted only two (of the eight reported) infringement actions against a state between 1880 and 1990. At most, Congress had heard there might be an increase in the future. The law did not respond to "a history of 'widespread and persisting deprivation of constitutional rights.'"

In the face of this puny showing of wrongs, the remedy was disproportionate. It subjected the states as infringers to triple damages and attorney's fees—unlike the United States itself, which was liable only for actual damages. It made the states liable for negligent as well as intentional violations. It made the states liable for contributory as well as direct infringement. It did not limit the federal remedy only to states with a high incidence of infringement. In fine, the statute treated the states no better than an infringing corporation. Worse, Congress had only taken a perfunctory look at what the states themselves had to offer in the way of remedy for their own actions. Was a federal remedy appropriate, it was implicitly asked, if state remedies were available? The disproportion of the sweeping federal remedy was not bearable. The patent law of the United States, in force since 1790, was unconstitutional as it bore upon the states.

The case divided the court more closely than *Boerne*, where there was an undertone of umbrage at Congress correcting the court. Here, Congress had not corrected the court but obeyed the court's requirement that the abrogation of state sovereignty be explicit. Congress, the dissent suggested, should not be faulted for failing in 1992 to meet criteria only promulgated by the court in *Boerne* in 1997. In any case, the criteria had been met. Congress had heard testimony of patent infringement by states and the prediction that it would increase. Why should Congress have considered state remedies for such infringement when federal patent law preempted state law and prevented the states from offering remedies? As for the proportion of the legislation to the evil perceived, if there were few state infringements, there would be few lawsuits; if there were many infringements, there would be many suits. What proportion could be more exact?

Even within the framework erected by *Boerne*, a further observation could be made beyond the points made by the dissent. Was it reasonable to expect "widespread and persistent deprivation" by the states of patent rights, when, since 1790, federal law had protected patentees? What was the point of hypothetically speaking of states with a high incidence of infringement when of course no states had repeatedly disregarded what was apparently binding federal law? It would have been a bold and lawless state that would have intentionally violated the patent law in force, risking in modern times the payment of triple damages. To suggest, as the court's opinion did, that only a history of wrongs justified Congress acting to protect property was to set a standard that could only be met in the future, when it was seen what the states and their auxiliary institutions would do in the absence of damages enforceable against them. At the same time the court's insistence on a history of wrongs meant that Congress could only enact remedial legislation. Laws that anticipated evils and prevented them could not be enacted to protect property.

Patents were a peculiar kind of property—property that existed only by act of Congress. But for the patent laws, an inventor's invention could be appropriated by anyone. It was seriously argued by the Education Expense Board that if Congress had the power to create property and protect it by the fourteenth amendment, Congress could do an end run around the restrictions on its article I powers. The argument was mistaken. The only property Congress had power to make was property in the patents and copyrights it authorized. To say that this property could not be protected by suit against the state was to impair a power of Congress explicitly given to it by the constitution. To intimate, as the court did, that federal patentees could still claim that the patents bound the states, and that the states should recognize this claim, was to announce that the patentees had a right to an injunction but not to damages—a mutilated kind of right to property.

To suggest, as the court also did, that a patentee might be able to find a remedy in a state court was unhelpful. Existing patent law largely preempted the state courts. They could not furnish much of a remedy.

In the case of the right to an abortion, the Supreme Court had explained its adherence to precedent by emphasizing the reliance of millions of persons on the availability of abortion. The court now did not mention the reliance of millions of patentees on the protection of the patent laws. The damage to them was treated not only as collateral but as so inconsequential as not to be worthy of mention.

Patents were a cherished creation of the constitution; it had scarcely been thinkable that a hole could be made in their protection. There was only one word for the court's decision: bizarre. "Truly bizarre," said Charles Fried, solicitor general of the United States in the Reagan administration. "Bizarre," said James N. Gardner, a senior patent attorney at Gardner & Garner, P.C., attorneys of Portland, Oregon. "Bizarre," repeated *Science*, the organ of the American Association for the Advancement of Science. None of these authorities in their respective worlds of constitutional law, patent law, and scientific research had expected the criteria of *Boerne* to reach out and wrench away a section of federal law in place for over two centuries. The consequences for "IP-dependent sectors of the American economy like biotechnology, software, entertainment, and pharmaceutical manufacturing" were seen "as potentially devastating."

The decision also affected the obligations of the United States as a member of the World Trade Organization (WTO). The Marrakesh Agreement of April 15, 1994 established the WTO with an accompanying agreement on Trade-Related Aspects of Intellectual Property Rights (TRIPS). TRIPS limited any use of a patent "by the government or third parties" and specified that "adequate remuneration in the circumstances of the case" must be provided the patentee. Nothing like the lack of protection for the patentee from the infringements of fifty states and their auxiliaries appears to have been anticipated by the agreement. The dispute mechanism set up by TRIPS would be necessary to resolve the responsibility of the United States if another nation complained that its patents were being appropriated by a state.

THE EVIL OF STATE ACCOUNTABILITY

The companion case begun by CSB alleged false advertising by the Education Expense Board. At first the board defended on the merits, but after *Seminole Tribe* was decided, holding that Congress could not pierce state immunity by exercising the federal power to regulate interstate commerce, the board stood on its sovereignty. The district court dismissed the suit, and the Third Circuit affirmed. But the case became a battleground in the Supreme Court.

Congress had specifically abrogated state immunity to Lanham Act suits, but this legislation, the Trademark Remedy Clarification Act of 1992, was treated as invalid as Congress's similar abrogation of immunity to patent suits. For the majority, the case was a simple application of the eleventh amendment to a suit by an out-of-state plaintiff against the state of Florida. *Seminole Tribe* controlled. It was irrelevant that the state was acting for profit and might be competing unfairly with private persons. "Evenhandedness" could not be expected. "In contrast, a suit against an unconsenting State is the very evil at which the Eleventh Amendment is directed."

The vehemence of the court, describing a suit against a state as an evil, underlined what the court was not admitting to be an injustice—that an individual had a right without a remedy. The intensity of the court's commitment to immunity was further emphasized by the opinion of the court declaring that the dissent's view that the protection of liberty was "promoted by the sharing among citizens of governmental decisionmaking authority" expressed a sentiment that "might well have dropped from the lips of Robespierre." The comparison of the words of four members of the court to the thought of the violent French demagogue strained judicial civility to its breaking point.

As to the power of Congress under the fourteenth amendment, the court did not even get to an inspection of the record before Congress. Rather, the court held that the right to be free of unfair competition was not "property." As it was not property, the right was beyond the protection of Congress exercising its section 5 power.

The four dissenters, now embattled in determination not to let immunity sweep away acts of Congress governing commerce, argued that when a state engaged "in ordinary commercial ventures," it subjected itself to federal regulation. One dissenter added that if eighteenth-century assumptions about immunity were to animate the court, then the immunity of a state should not be greater than that of a foreign sovereign. Under the Foreign Sovereign Immunities Act, that immunity did not extend to a foreign government's "commercial activity."

The dissent's questioning of immunity for commercial enterprises of the state may have contributed to the irritability of the court. The questioning touched on an extension of sovereign immunity that the court had never attempted to explain or justify. The question was answered here only by citation of a 1920 case in which the state of New York had been held immune in its operation of a ferry. The rationale for immunity favored by the court—the dignity of the sovereign—seemed singularly ill-matched to either a ferry or an insurance scheme.

THE TRIVIALITY OF TRADEMARKS

There are over one million trademarks registered with the Office of Patents and Copyrights. CSB did not put its trademark to the test in suing the Education Expense Board. If it had, there is no reason to believe that the result would have been different than for its patent. Under the court's reasoning, *Seminole Tribe* prevented Congress from protecting a trademark under article I, and it is unlikely that the congressional record of an evil to be prevented would have been better than the record regarding patents that was found wanting. No case has been found since *College Savings Bank* where a state has been successfully sued for infringement of a trademark.

THE UNLIKELY LIGHTNESS
OF COPYRIGHT PROTECTION

Could copyright be treated differently? Denise Chávez, a playwright and novelist of the southwest, was to find out. In 1984, she contracted with Arte Publico Press for it to publish a collection of her short stories, *The Last of the Menu Girls*, whose title story drew on her own experience as a young hospital intern, bringing the day's menu to patients. Arte Publico had been founded in 1979 in Gary, Indiana, by Nicholás Kanellos. The following year, Kanellos was invited to teach Hispanic literature at the University of Houston and to bring Arte Publico with him. Chávez and Arte Publico appeared to be a good match. The book was popular enough to warrant reprinting. Chávez, however, was dissatisfied with misprints in the first edition and by Arte Publico's failure to correct them. She declined to permit further publication and in 1993 sued Arte Publico when it proceeded to publish anyway.

Arte Publico pleaded immunity. It was operated by the University of Houston and sought to be identified with the university, which in turn sought to be identified with the state of Texas. The district court accepted the identifications. As an arm of the state, the press wore the state's mantle of immunity. But Congress by the Copyright Remedy Clarification Act of 1992 had abrogated the states' immunity in the same way it had abrogated their immunity from patent suits, so the district court rejected the claim of immunity. The Fifth Circuit Court of Appeals affirmed. In 1996, the Supreme Court granted certiorari and remanded "for further consideration in light of *Seminole Tribe*," a broad hint that immunity might be in order.

On remand, the interest of the case was reflected in the Association of American Publishers, the Authors Guild, the American Society of Composers, Authors and Publishers, and a dozen other associations filing briefs as friends of the court. Writing for the circuit, Edith Jones, joined by Emilio Garza, took the Supreme Court's hint with enthusiasm. *Seminole Tribe* applied and so Congress could not use its power under article I. As for its power under section 5 of the fourteenth amendment, *Boerne* required that the power be used to remedy an evil, and the court, looking only at the absence of copyright litigation against the states, thought that there had been no evil to be remedied.

John Minor Wisdom, at age ninety-two one of the most respected of federal judges, dissented from the panel's holding. Had the Supreme Court really meant to be so sweeping in *Boerne*? "Are you so sure?" he asked his colleagues. The Fifth Circuit voted to take the case en banc. While the case was waiting oral argument, the Supreme Court decided *College Savings Bank*. Chávez's case was returned to the panel, which now unanimously followed the pattern so clearly set by the Supreme Court. The panel relied, in particular, on testimony before Congress that the states were "all respectful of the copyright laws." Only a potential for future abuse had been identified. There was nothing to indicate "the kind of massive constitutional violations that have prompted proper remedial legislation." Chávez's claim for money damages was dismissed.

Chávez v. Arte Publico Press was a perfect illustration of the impact of the *Boerne* criteria on the federal system. There was no effort to confine the immunity to the core functions of government. A dependency of a dependency of the state qualified as immune. Now it was no longer the Supreme Court that examined the congressional record and found Congress's efforts flawed if the record was light. It was a circuit court, and, by implication, it could be any federal district court. The federal judiciary as a whole was to function as the censor of Congress. Following *College Savings Bank*, the system would brush aside the preventative power of Congress under the fourteenth amendment. Massive past violations would have to be established.

The topsy-turvy shift in roles between Congress and the courts was not emphasized by the courts, but inhered in the decisions. The Supreme Court could announce a new constitutional rule binding the entire country on the record made in a single case. Congress could not make a new rule absent a record of multiple and persistent violations of the constitution over a period of time.

The Library of Congress contains 115 million items in a variety of formats. It's a fair estimate that over 100 million carry copyrights that are still valid. As the Supreme Court had ignored the expectations of patentees, so now the circuit court ignored the expectations of the copyright owners. Who among them would have thought that the federal courts would cease to be the zealous protectors of their property? No author contracting with the press of a state university in 1984 would have imagined that the copyright retained by the author could be disregarded by the press. No author would have suspected that if she sued the press, her case for damages could be barred from federal court without a trial. Even today, in 2001, few authors whose books are being published by a state university press would be likely to know that a reservation of copyright to the author could not be protected by a suit for damages if the publisher chose to disregard the copyright. But *Boerne* and *College Savings Bank* now ruled the worlds of patent, copyright, and trademark. Beyond intellectual property, what other domains would be immune if occupied by a state or its surrogate?

CHAPTER 5

Perhaps Inconsequential Problems

PROBABLY UNTRUE BUT RATIONALLY CONCEIVABLE STEREOTYPES

Age is an easy and obvious way by which people may be classified. School age and voting age are fixed by law; retirement age often has been. Distinctions of this kind appear to be natural and unavoidable, necessary for the functioning of society, and not invidious. Like any system of classification, they submerge the individual in the group and fail to recognize exceptions. They suppose the stereotypical. They act on the basis of the average. When the individual is merged in the average, does the individual suffer a loss of civil rights?

In 1964, in the course of enacting the Civil Rights Act, Congress directed the secretary of labor to report on the extent of employment discrimination based on age and to recommend legislation to prevent "arbitrary discrimination" on account of age. Although not finding a prevalent animus against the old, the secretary reported a preference for the young. He noted that a study of five hundred employers in five cities around the country showed almost 60 percent had an age limit beyond which they would not hire. Youth was preferred because of superior physical abilities and health, educational level, and easier fit within pension plans. The secretary was cautious about the effect of arbitrary discrimination but suggested that it had a substantial cost in the loss of productive workers and a palpable impact on the individuals affected. The secretary recommended federal legislation to eliminate the arbitrary use of age.

The secretary's report led in 1967 to the Age Discrimination in Employment Act (ADEA). The law had been recommended by President Johnson in "Older Americans," a message to Congress emphasizing the "hundreds of thousands" unemployed "because of arbitrary age discrimination." Twenty-four states already prohibited such discrimination to some degree. It was time, the president said, to treat it as a national problem. The bill passed both the House and the Senate by unanimous consent. The ADEA covered firing or failing to hire an employee because of age, with exceptions for bona fide occupational requirements. It covered only those between forty and sixty-five, only employers of twenty or more, and only nongovernmental employees.

In 1972, not coincidentally a presidential election year, "ageism" as a term of opprobrium was given presidential recognition. In a message to Congress, President Nixon declared that ageism "can be as great an evil in our society as discrimination based on race or religion or any other characteristic which ignores a person's unique status as an individual and treats him or her as a member of some arbitrarily defined group." This passage implicitly attacked age as an arbitrary classifier, at least for those in the work force, and reflected a philosophy that saw each person as unique, with a uniqueness not to be squashed by stereotypes. The president recommended extending the ADEA to government employees.

No legislation resulted immediately. In 1973, the creation by the Senate of a Special Committee on the Ageing reflected the increasing political power of older Americans. A working paper for the committee, entitled "Improving the Age Discrimination Law," reported that the Department of Labor had filed 140 suits charging age discrimination and that, of over six thousand business establishments investigated by the department in 1972, 36 percent had been in violation of the ADEA. A number of corporate managers, the report asserted anecdotally, still thought preference for younger employees was "a good idea" and saw age discrimination as "a fact of corporate life."

In 1974, the presidential message of 1972 was called to mind by Congress and followed. It was explained in the committee report that the omission of governmental employees in 1967 was not "a conscious decision," but had come about because they fell outside the Fair Labor Standards Act and so were outside the enforcement powers of the Department of Labor, ADEA's designated enforcer. The Fair Labor Standards Act was now amended to include "a State or political subdivision of a State and any agency or instrumentality of a State or a political subdivision of a State." The legislation passed 375 to 37 in the House and 71 to 19 in the Senate and was signed into law by President Ford.

Among the several smaller worlds affected by the change, none had more interest in it than the world of state colleges and universities characterized by mandatory retirement ages based partly on stereotypes of intellectual vigor declining with age, partly on a preference for periodic injections of fresh thinking. After extending the ADEA to cover public employees, Congress enacted the law in 1978, barring mandatory retirement for those covered by the ADEA, at that time all those under the age of seventy. In 1986, the ADEA was again amended to eliminate the upper age above which the protections of the act did not extend. The 1986 amendment contained an exemption for tenured professors, who could still be subject to mandatory retirement but only until 1994.

Roderick MacPherson and Marvin Narz were faculty at the College of Business of the University of Montevallo, a part of the educational system of the state of Alabama located in Shelby County, Alabama. Each was an associate professor who had not been promoted. Each believed that his age had led to discriminatory evaluations of his ability. In 1994, MacPherson, aged fifty-seven, and Narz, aged fifty-eight, sued Montevallo. The university claimed the immunity of the state. Judge William H. Acker Jr., of the district court for Northern Alabama, dismissed the suit.

In 1995, J. Daniel Kimel, a faculty member at Florida State University, sued the Florida Board of Regents for age discrimination. A group of other faculty and librarians became co-plaintiffs and were later joined by other faculty and librarians from Florida International University, another university of the state. All at ages above forty, the plaintiffs asserted that the state system had not allocated funds to provide agreed-on salary adjustments and that this failure had discriminated against older employees of the system. Judge Maurice M. Paul for the Tallahassee Division of the district court for Northern Florida refused to dismiss the suit. Also in 1996, Wellington Dickson sued in the Panama City Division of this district court, asserting that his employer, the Florida Department of Corrections, had failed to promote him to sergeant because of his age. Judge Robert L. Hinkle permitted Dickson's suit to proceed.

Appeals in all three cases were taken to the Eleventh Circuit Court of Appeals. The solicitor general of the United States intervened to defend the antidiscrimination law. Chief Judge Joseph W. Hatchett thought none of the defendants was immune. Judge James L. Edmondson doubted that Congress had meant to abrogate the states' immunity. Judge Emmett Ripley Cox thought that the ADEA as applied to the states was "not a proportional response to any widespread violation of the elderly's constitutional rights." The legislation, in his view, went well beyond what the constitution as interpreted by the Supreme Court required. The legislative sponsors hadn't mentioned the constitution at all, but had "simply thought it [the law] was a good idea." The circuit court, two to one, dismissed the three cases.

Taking this position, the Eleventh Circuit joined the Eighth Circuit, which had held the University of Minnesota immune. Six other circuits—the Second, the Fifth, the Sixth, the Seventh, the Ninth, and the Tenth—had ruled to the contrary. In the face of this split among the circuits, it was easy for the Supreme Court to decide to grant certiorari, and the court picked the three appeals from the Eleventh to decide the issue for the country.

The structure of decision for the national court was set by *Seminole*, *Boerne*, and *College Savings Bank*. Congress, in the exercise of its article I power over interstate commerce, could make a standard applicable to the fifty states but could not make the states amenable to suits for damages by individuals claiming the protection of the standard. Congress could only make the states suable by exercising its fourteenth amendment, section 5 power. To do that, Congress had to abrogate the states' immunity. Then it had to act on a record establishing an evil and devise a commensurate and proportionate response. Congress had specifically stated that states were not immune from suits under the ADEA (two justices found the act ambiguous and so disagreed with the abrogation of immunity). But once again Congress had failed the *Boerne* tests. The evil had not been established. The legislative response was disproportionate. The states remained immune.

The point of departure for the court was its own teaching on age discrimination. The court had already held that states did not violate the constitution if there was a rational basis for the line they drew based on age. It was alright for Massachusetts to require state police to retire at fifty— relative youth was a qualification for the job. It was alright for Missouri to require state judges to retire at seventy. It was, the court had said, "an unfortunate fact of life that physical and mental capacities sometimes diminish with age," so "the people may therefore wish to replace some older judges." The Supreme Court, all of whose members were, in ADEA terms, "older judges," had gone on to say, "It is far from true that all judges suffer significant deterioration in performance at age 70. It is probably not true that most do. It may not be true at all." But what was probably not true could "reasonably be conceived to be true" by the state decision makers. That reasonable conception was sufficient to insulate the Missouri age limit from constitutional invalidity.

Against this backdrop of court-made constitutional law, Congress had gone too far in making all discrimination against the elderly unlawful. True, Congress had made an exception for jobs that required younger persons, but the exception had been narrowed by the court itself to jobs where youth was not merely a reasonable requirement, but a requirement of "reasonable necessity." So interpreted, the ADEA set a universal standard higher than the court set as a constitutional requirement, and only what was a constitutional requirement could be imposed on the states. Congress could not go beyond the court's constitutional standard and impose "substantially higher burdens on state employers."

In the light of the court's constitutional standard, Congress had not "identified any pattern of age discrimination" by the states; much less had it identified "any discrimination that rose to the level of constitutional violation." The evidence before Congress had been newspaper articles about federal employees and letters from constituents to senators, plus a 1966 report prepared by the state of California pointing to age discrimination by its public agencies. But the discrimination that California had documented was rational discrimination allowed by California law and by the ADEA itself; even if California had shown unconstitutional discrimination by California, its failings would not justify extension of the ADEA to all fifty states. In sum, "Congress had virtually no reason to believe that state and local governments were unconstitutionally discriminating against their employees on the basis of age." Therefore the court held that "the ADEA is not a valid exercise of Congress' power under § 5 of the fourteenth amendment." The ADEA, applied to the states, was "an unwarranted response to a perhaps inconsequential problem."

Congress had passed the Age Discrimination in Employment Act and extended it to the 4.5 million employees of the states in entire innocence. Unknowing of, and unsuspecting, the *Boerne* criteria that would be announced years later, Congress had acted in 1967, 1974, 1978, and 1986 like all legislatures act most of the time. An organized constituency had told the members that there was a problem. The members' own experiences were not to the contrary. Two presidents told them that there was a serious evil to be remedied. Both major parties agreed that solutions were needed. The legislature responded to its constituents, its own experience, its leaders, the major parties, and to the absence of much opposition. Congress did not build a record the way a trial judge builds a record that will sustain scrutiny by an appellate court. The criteria of *Boerne* retroactively invalidated the legislation.

The court again split, five to four, with the same dissenters as in *College Savings Bank*. Explicitly reproved by the court for not accepting the recent precedents, the dissenters defended themselves against the reproof. The lead case limiting Congress's power under article I, *Seminole*, was so "profoundly misguided" that it did not deserve respect as binding precedent. Moreover, in the interpretation of the constitution, there was less force in the rule of stare decisis because, as Brandeis had pointed out long ago, the court frequently changed its mind on constitutional questions and rightly so, given the difficulty of correcting the court's mistakes by amendment of the constitution. In the area of law under consideration here, the court "by its own re-peated overruling of earlier precedent" had itself discounted the importance of precedent. Finally, there could be no reliance by the fifty states on immunity, because they knew that the federal government itself could bring them into court and force their obedience to the federal standard. As Congress could set the standard, and the federal government could sue to enforce the standard, it was a question of political judgment whether indi-viduals should also be allowed to sue the states. The Supreme Court had no business making this "policy choice," which was Congress's to make. The dissent did not attack the *Boerne* crite-ria that crippled Congress. The dissent avoided *Boerne* by argu-ing that article I power was adequate for Congress's decision to make the states suable.

Beyond the dissenters' critique, the opinion of the court on its own terms deserves comment. Twice the court complained of the burden placed on local governments. But local governments were not before the court, and the fourteenth amendment re-stricted action by the states, not cities. The court repeated *Boerne* that Congress had "wide latitude" in enforcing the guarantees of the fourteenth amendment. The court noted that Congress could enact "reasonably prophylactic legislation." The exercise of section 5 power by Congress was "entitled to much defer-ence." But these generalities were subverted by the court's close scrutiny of the evidence on which Congress had acted and by the court's measuring of the proportionality of the legislation to the evil established. Congress, the court said, was not confined to law "that merely parrots the precise working" of the fourteenth amendment; Congress could forbid "a somewhat broader swath of conduct." A "swath" refers metaphorically to the path cut by a scythe. The scythe that the court would let Congress cut with, and the path it could cut, were scarcely clear when the swath was vaguely qualified as "somewhat broader." The court alone decided how broad the cut could be.

As to the ADEA, the court thought Congress had addressed a maybe inconsequential problem. But by virtue of the litigation before the court and the circuits, the court had to be aware that many state universities and colleges forced retirement of elderly faculty. Was this problem of higher education of no consequence? Or was it to be dismissed, like the forced retirement of judges, as based on a belief in the decline of mental vigor with advance in age, a belief that, although probably not true, could rationally be conceived to be true?

More fundamental, how reasonable was it for the court to rely on what could "rationally" be believed about the effect of age? At one time in American history, Thomas Jefferson, surely a rational person, had believed in the inferiority of African Americans. He had accepted a prevalent stereotype that fed irrational prejudice. Was the stereotype of the intellectually declining person of seventy or sixty-five anything different? Why should what was "probably not true" be taken as the basis for discrimination treated as rational?

Bowing to the stereotype of the elderly, the court unwittingly demonstrated the prevalence of the stereotype throughout the land. If the court itself thought the stereotype a reasonable belief, could not anyone conclude that the prejudice was pretty universal? Faulting Congress for not documenting specific acts of discrimination by the states, the court overlooked what Congress had demonstrated: that, throughout American society, employment discrimination against the elderly was widespread. On what basis could the court conclude that Congress was mistaken when it assumed that the states as employers behaved like other employers and discriminated on account of age?

The court itself was, perhaps, the least representative body in America to judge of the existence of discrimination based on age. At the time of the court's pronouncement on the ADEA, its members ranged in age from fifty-one to seventy-nine. Each member was protected by article III of the constitution guaranteeing each justice life tenure unless impeached. If a member retired, the annuity on retirement equaled the salary being paid. Secure in their employment and their income, the members of the court had no personal experience of the bite of age discrimination and could not expect to have experience of it. They judged the possible inconsequentialness of forced retirement with the serenity of observers who would never undergo it.

From this vantage point, the court went out of its way to say that the elderly were not "a discrete and insular minority." This classic phrase, first inserted in a footnote in *Carolene Products* in the 1930s, was the description of any group likely to be the subject of discrimination, unable to protect itself in the political process, and so deserving of the special solicitude of the court. It was true that the Indian tribes trying to protect their burial grounds, as well as the members of the Native American religion, had been members of discrete and insular minorities and had not received any help from the court. Still, the phrase, familiar to every law student, had an evocative resonance. If the elderly were not a discrete and insular minority, the court implied, there was no reason to come to their assistance with the ADEA. And they were not, the court reasoned, because "all persons, if they live out their normal life spans, will experience it." "It" was "old age."

How insensitive to human experience that truism was as a reason for denying the minority status of the aged. At any given time, the majority of persons are not old. That someday those persons will be old is almost as small a restraint upon their beliefs and actions as the knowledge that they once had lived in wombs impels them to reject abortion. That was then, old age comes in the future, this is now, so human experience suggests that human beings reason. All the laws and practices of the society at large that required compulsory retirement at a given age, all the laws and practices that justified the ADEA as rational legislation for private employers, demonstrated that the majority looked at those it could conveniently catalog as old and treated them differently and worse. If the majority stuck together, the discrete and insular minority of the old could do little about it.

THE STRIKINGLY FAMILIAR FEEL OF THE ELEVENTH AMENDMENT

With the decisions of *College Savings Bank* and *Kimel* in 1999, it was evident to all observers of the court that the battle of *Boerne* had been but the opening encounter in what had now become a continuing struggle between an innovative and entrenched group of five justices committed to an agenda controlled by sovereign immunity and a minority, one vote short, attempting to defend positions once believed to be established. In 2000, the Americans with Disabilities Act (ADA) was where the two sides clashed.

When Congress enacted the ADA in 1990, it began the statute with the finding that 43 million Americans have one or more physical or mental disabilities and that "historically, society has tended to isolate and segregate individuals with disabilities." Discrimination against such individuals was "a serious and pervasive social problem," persisting in employment, housing, public accommodations, education, transportation, communication, recreation, institutionalization, health services, voting, and access to public services. The disabled, Congress found, were "a discrete and insular minority" with their status "based on characteristics that go beyond the control of such individuals" and determined by "stereotypic assumptions."

As early as 1920, Congress had legislated in aid of the disabled. The pace of legislation had picked up in the late 1960s, and by 1988 ten federal acts were in place partially protecting the disabled. In 1988, Congress created the Task Force on the Rights and Empowerment of Americans with Disabilities, which held hearings in every state and heard the testimony of thousands of disabled individuals who had suffered discriminatory acts. At the conclusion of this process, the task force chairman, Justin Dart, testified that the discrimination was "massive, society-wide."

Congress itself over a two-year period held nineteen hearings before House or Senate committees that took testimony from the disabled, their advocacy organizations, and academic experts. Congress confirmed its sense of society's crippling stereotypes by national opinion polls and by census data on the disabled. Drawing on all this information and on its members' own experience of life in the United States, Congress made the findings that formed the first part of the statute enacted in 1990. What

Congress did not do was to specify that the fifty states themselves violated the rights of the disabled. The omission was obvious when in 2000 the ADA, as applied to state employers, came before the Supreme Court.

Patricia Garrett had begun work in 1977 at University of Alabama Hospital in Birmingham as a registered nurse. By 1994, aged fifty-six, she had been promoted to director of nursing, OB/Gyn/Neonatal Services. In September 1994, she was diagnosed as having breast cancer. She underwent lumpectomy, radiation, and chemotherapy. According to Garrett, her supervisor, Sabrina Shannon, the hospital's associate executive director, initially encouraged, then pressured her to take leave or transfer to a lesser job. Shannon had Garrett's old job listed as open. Garrett found herself locked out of the hospital's computer systems. When she described these events to her doctor in March 1995, he warned her that workplace harassment was harmful to her health. She took leave and returned to work in July 1995. Shannon told her she was not wanted back. At the insistence of the personnel department, she was allowed back but found her supervisor so critical that she accepted a transfer to a convalescent hospital at a $13,000 cut in compensation. She sued the hospital under the ADA.

A separate suit was brought by Milton Ash, a security officer in the Alabama Department of Youth Services since 1993. He suffered from chronic asthma and sleep apnea. He requested the department to enforce its no-smoking rule in the small gatehouse where he worked and to fix the departmental vehicles he rode so that carbon monoxide would not be emitted within them. The department did not respond. Ash complained to the Equal Employment Opportunity Commission. His performance ratings were lowered. He sued the department in the district court for northern Alabama.

District Judge William M. Acker Jr. dismissed both suits on the ground of the sovereign immunity of the defendants. The cases were consolidated on appeal to the Eleventh Circuit, which held that Congress in the ADA had unequivocally abrogated state immunity. The court did not go on to address the proportionality of the statute. The district court was reversed. The defendants sought certiorari and got it from the Supreme Court.

As the hour of judgment came for the ADA and state employees, the solicitor general of the United States defended the statute, and organizations that had helped to pass it filed briefs as amici. They included Self-Advocates Becoming Empowered; the National Association of Protection and Advocacy Systems; and the United Cerebral Palsy Association.

Ominously for Garrett and Ash, the opinion of the court began with a recitation of the text of the eleventh amendment followed by this declaration:

> Although by its terms the Amendment applies only to suits
> against a State by citizens of another State, our cases have
> extended the Amendment's applicability to suits by citizens
> against their own State.... The ultimate guarantee of the
> Eleventh Amendment is that non-consenting States may
> not be sued by private individuals in federal court.

The court-created doctrine of the sovereign immunity of the states was now formally equated with a text in the constitution, said to guarantee this immunity. Congress could abrogate that immunity by properly using its section 5 power under the fourteenth amendment. Proper use required conformity with the criteria of *Boerne*. The court went on to apply "these now familiar principles."

Under the court's precedents, discrimination against the disabled was not unconstitutional if the discrimination had a rational basis. The legislative record, the court said, "simply fails to show that Congress did in fact identify a pattern of irrational state discrimination against the disabled." At most, the court's attention had been directed by the litigants to "half a dozen examples" where a state was involved, and even in these cases it was debatable whether the states' acts of discrimination had been irrational. The committee reports of House and Senate mentioned discrimination by private employers but not by states, suggesting that "no pattern of unconstitutional state discrimination had been documented."

Even if it were possible "to squeeze out of these examples" a pattern, the ADA was a disproportionate remedy. The ADA's requirement that facilities used by employees be made accessible to the disabled went beyond what "the constitution," i.e., the court, required from a rational state employer. The ADA, moreover, put the burden on the employer to show that a modification of facilities would impose an "undue hardship." The constitution, i.e., the court, put the burden on the employee. In a word, Congress had gone farther than the court, the evil of a discriminatory pattern by the states had not been proved, and Congress's response had not been congruent and proportionate. The ADA, as applied to state employees, was unconstitutional.

The four dissenters evaluated the evidence before Congress differently. If the evidence showed massive discrimination by private employers and by municipalities, there was no reason to believe that the states were free from the stereotypical assumptions that were prevalent in the society as a whole. Moreover, the legislative record contained not a half dozen examples but "roughly 300" cases of discrimination by states. The three hundred were listed in an appendix to the dissent, with each state of the Union heading a summary list of all the state's acts of discrimination, from inaccessible exercise equipment at the University of Alabama to inaccessible state buildings in Wyoming. Acts of actual employment discrimination were not many, and the incidents listed did not show that the discrimination lacked justification. "But," the dissent observed, "a legislature is not a court of law." A legislature drew general conclusions from anecdotes and opinion evidence. The legislature was free to draw such conclusions, especially when "strong refutation" was lacking. Traditionally, the court had never required Congress to break down the evidence before it, category by category.

The court had it backwards, the dissent continued, when the court put the burden on Congress to prove that its legislation was justified. The burden was on those challenging the law. "Unlike courts, Congress directly reflects public attitudes and beliefs, enabling Congress better to understand where, and to what extent," refusal to accommodate a disability was unjustified. The court, holding the ADA unconstitutional, supposed that many state discriminations were rationally justified; but such a presumption of rationality was to guide courts reviewing legislation, not Congress viewing the practices of the nation. The court was standing principle "on its head."

The dissent went on to challenge the court's test of what was "congruent." A congruent remedy could exceed what the constitution by itself required. Under section 5 of the fourteenth amendment, Congress had the power to do all that was appropriate to achieve its objective. Congress could use any rational means that had a tendency to effectuate the constitutional principle of equal treatment.

The spirit of John Marshall spoke in the dissent. And, the majority was reminded, first, that while the court had repeatedly in recent cases spoken of its deference to Congress, it did not show deference; and second, that its treatment of the section 5 power of Congress was "reminiscent" of the discredited limitation that the court in the 1930s had put on Congress's power over commerce. In conclusion, the court "improperly invades a power that the Constitution assigned to Congress."

Improperly weighing the evidence before Congress, denying the competence of Congress, turning principle topsy-turvy, invading a domain assigned by the constitution to the legislature— the dissent's indictment of the court reflected the degree to which the court had departed from precedent to keep the states from being sued. The continuing division in the court was a measure of the magnitude of the shift in the middle ground where the power of the nation was being narrowed.

CHAPTER 6

Gang Rape at State U.

Ever since *Seminole Tribe* in 1996, the Supreme Court had been moving to reduce the accountability of the states for not complying with federal legislation. A new issue was presented when federal legislation was enacted to remedy a perceived failure in the states' ordinary administration of criminal justice—when, observing this failure, Congress declared that "all persons within the United States shall have the right to be free from crimes of violence motivated by gender" and provided for a civil action for damages against any perpetrator of such a crime. The Violence Against Women Act was passed in 1994. It came before the court in 1999.

Christy Brzonkala, age eighteen, began her freshman year at Virginia Polytechnic Institute and State University in the fall of 1994. As she told her story, she had been recruited as a student athlete and as a prospect for the women's softball team. Within a month of her arrival at Virginia Tech, she met in her dormitory two members of the varsity football team, Antonio Morrison and James Crawford, and within thirty minutes of meeting her, they raped her—first Morrison, then Crawford, then Morrison again. As Morrison left, he expressed the earnest hope that Christy had no communicable diseases. At the time she did not even know their names, only that they were on the football team. Emotionally shattered, she stopped attending classes and even attempted to kill herself. A psychiatrist licensed by the school treated her with antidepressant pills. No representative of Virginia Tech made more than a cursory inquiry about the reason for her distress. Eventually she withdrew from the school. She brought no criminal charges against the football players.

In early 1995, Christy Brzonkala returned to the campus and complained to the institute about Morrison's and Crawford's conduct. In the dormitory dining hall Morrison had been heard to boast of his modus operandi with women—first get them drunk, then have sex. At a school disciplinary hearing, Morrison admitted having sexual contact and agreed that Brzonkala had twice said, "No." The Judicial Committee of the school acquitted Crawford and found Morrison guilty of sexual assault. He was suspended for two semesters.

Morrison announced that he intended to challenge this verdict in court, in part on the ground that Virginia Tech had punished him under a Sexual Assault Policy which had not been included in the Student Handbook, although it had been issued in June 1994. Virginia Tech had already defended itself in another case against such a due process objection, and the objection had proved groundless. However, two female employees made the four-hour drive to Brzonkala's home in the summer to persuade her that it was "technically" necessary to have a new hearing. Virginia Tech proceeded to hold one. Morrison was now tried under the Abusive Conduct Policy, which had been in force earlier. The committee ruled that student testimony at the first hearing could not be made part of the record; Brzonkala would have to obtain affidavits from those who testified before— a requirement she could not meet because the students were scattered on summer break. Virginia Tech denied her access to audiotape and other records of the hearing, while granting Morrison and his lawyer full access. Again he was sentenced to two semesters' suspension, but his misconduct was now described as one of "using abusive language."

Morrison's offense, it had turned out, was linguistic. He had used "fucking" as an intensifier to describe the social diseases he hoped Brzonkala did not have. In his dining room boast, he had said he liked to "fuck" women. These words were the subject of his censure. That they were the common or garden-variety usage of many young men of his generation was ignored. Shifting the focus to what he had said from what he had done, the committee trivialized his action.

Morrison appealed his sentence to higher officials of the university. No notice was given Brzonkala. The provost, Peggy Meszaros, found Morrison's sentence "excessive when compared with other cases" and annulled it. Morrison was free to return to Virginia Tech in the fall of 1995. He did return, on a full athletic scholarship. The result, Brzonkala believed, was due to the influence of the head football coach, who wanted Morrison back for the season. When she learned of his plan to return, she again withdrew.

Virginia Tech is a state university in Blacksburg, Virginia, with over twenty thousand undergraduate and graduate students, 60 percent of them men and 40 percent of them women. In a statistical report that was publicly available, Virginia Tech noted that between 1992 and 1993 it had through internal proceedings adjudicated thirteen rapes, nine resulting in some form of discipline of the accused assailant; in none was any action by the police indicated. Virginia Tech did not report Brzonkala's charges to the police. Virginia Tech has a fine reputation as a football power. In 1995, it was to rank eighth in the nation.

Under Virginia law, rape is a crime with a remarkably wide range of sanctions, from five years to life imprisonment, the choice being left to "the discretion of the court or the jury." At all events, it is a felony, and the penalty prescribed by the law is more than loss of a semester or two at school. Rape of a woman is the only violent felony that Virginia Tech does not automatically report to the police. In December 1995, Christy Brzonkala sued Morrison and Crawford for damages under the Violence Against Women Act, enacted into law on September 13, 1994, one week before the assault on her.

If Brzonkala's case was as strong as it was described in her pleadings, her case was a textbook example of why the Violence Against Women Act was needed. An eighteen-year-old woman studying at a state university, she had been raped on a state campus by two members of a male team, to whom the state institution gave procedural advantages it denied her. The institution had done little to sanction her assailants. It had not even counseled her to contact the police. It had either disbelieved her or not thought that a criminal violation of Virginia law against rape was sufficient grounds for seriously disciplining a student.

Although it knew that the basis of Morrison's threatened appeal was groundless, it had caved before his empty threat.

Brzonkala also sued Virginia Tech itself for discrimination based on sex in violation of Title IX of the Education Act of 1972. Jackson L. Kiser, chief judge for the Western District of Virginia, sitting in Roanoke, heard this case. He held that Brzonkala's allegations did not show sex discrimination; indeed her allegation that Virginia Tech influenced the proceedings to keep Morrison on the football team was an admission by her that Virginia Tech was not discriminating on the basis of gender, it merely wanted a football player back in service. That Virginia Tech did not report rapes to the police was also no evidence of bias on its part. It could be guessed, the judge suggested, that Virginia Tech's reason was sensitivity to the feelings of the victims of the rapes. The preferential treatment of Morrison was not discrimination. He was a defendant, Brzonkala was merely a complaining witness. Nor had Virginia Tech created an environment actually hostile to Brzonkala. She only feared that the environment "might become abusive in the future." Chief Judge Kiser dismissed her case against Virginia Tech for failure to state a cause of action—that is, as he read her complaint, no discrimination based on sex was even alleged.

Two months later Kiser ruled on Brzonkala's case against Morrison and Crawford. The first question for the judge was whether Brzonkala had sufficiently alleged a crime "committed because of gender or on the basis of gender, and due, at least in part, to an animus based on the victim's gender," as the statute required. A judge who found Virginia Tech's favoritism for the football team no evidence of gender bias, and who thought that nonprosecution of rape was a chivalrous gesture toward the victims, might not have been expected to find rape to be a crime committed with an animus based on gender. Nonetheless, Judge Kiser concluded that Brzonkala had alleged a crime that met the terms of the new law. He took into account Morrison's lack of prior knowledge of her, his comment about sexual diseases, and his public boast; the judge added that the assault by Morrison and Crawford was a species of gang rape.

The judge turned to the constitutionality of the Violence Against Women Act. In 1995, the Supreme Court had held in *United States v. Lopez* that a law banning a firearm in a school zone went beyond Congress's power to regulate commerce: no commerce was involved in what was made a crime. Tracking the reasoning of *Lopez*, the judge held that the Violence Against Women Act could not be upheld under the commerce power; clearly rape was not commerce. It was equally, the judge ruled, beyond the section 5 power of Congress. The new statute reached only private conduct, in which state action was not involved. If a state did not give equal protection to women, the Violence Against Women Act would remedy the deficiency "purely by chance." The statute was not sustainable as enforcement of the fourteenth amendment. Christy Brzonkala's case was dismissed without a trial.

Apparently, in the eyes of the court, it was purely by chance that a case which the United States itself had now entered as an intervenor was the case before the court, and it was purely by chance that the pleadings set out a story of rape unredressed by the state authorities. Whether or not the Violence Against Women Act could be found constitutional in some other case, why was this not one case where the state's default of its duty cried out for a remedy?

The Fourth Circuit opinion on appeal was written by Diana Gribbon Motz of Baltimore, Maryland. Her opening paragraph struck a different note from Judge Kiser: "This case arises from a gang rape of a freshman at the Virginia Polytechnic Institute by two members of the football team, and the school's decision to impose only a nominal punishment on the rapists." The court went on to hold that "the rapes themselves created a hostile environment," which Virginia Tech was aware of and never remedied. A slap on the wrist for rape was not adequate punishment. Brzonkala's claim against the university was reinstated.

The circuit also held that Brzonkala had alleged a crime committed with gender bias; the district court was affirmed on this point and was reversed on its conclusions about the law's validity. Congress had established the impact of gender-based crimes on interstate commerce. The Violence Against Women Act was, therefore, constitutional. Brzonkala's case against the two men was reinstated. Judge Kenneth Hall concurred. Judge J. Michael Luttig of Alexandria, Virginia, dissented as to the constitutionality of the new law. Judge Kiser's "excellent legal analysis" had been "abidingly faithful" to the Supreme Court's decision in *Lopez;* the majority of the panel showed "bold intransigence" in declining to accept *Lopez* as dispositive.

The Fourth Circuit took the case en banc. Judge Luttig wrote for the majority, as the court voted, seven to four, to dismiss the suit against the men. In an opinion occupying sixty-four pages in the Federal Reporter, Luttig celebrated the "foundational principles of our constitution" that made Congress's exertion of power void. Chief Judge Harvey Wilkinson, concurring, pondered whether history did not suggest that judges needed to be restrained in gutting legal remedies provided by the democratic process, but decided that the judges could not "ignore the vast temptation on the part of Congress to attempt the solution of any and all of our problems." It was the judges' job, he indicated, to temper the temptation. Diana Motz, dissenting, stuck to her guns, in twenty-eight pages dissecting the majority opinion.

A cause célèbre, the case headed for the Supreme Court. For the majority of that court, the notion that Congress would federalize the law of rape, the most local of crimes, was abhorrent. But the court began its analysis with the "presumption of constitutionality" enjoyed by the statute. After all, Congress was "a coordinate branch of Government." There must be "a plain showing" that Congress had overstepped its bounds before the court invalidated a statute.

Congress had the power, enumerated in article I, section 8 of the constitution, to regulate commerce among the states. The power had expanded considerably in 1937 with *NLRB v. Jones & Laughlin Steel Corp.*, the decisive swing accepting the New Deal and repudiating the court's earlier position that labor relations did not fall within this power. Congress, it had to be recognized, had some "latitude" in determining what did fall within it. Congress could regulate those activities "that substantially affect interstate commerce."

But activity that Congress regulated for its substantive effect on commerce, the court said, must itself have a commercial character, it must be an economic activity of some kind. Gender-related crime did not have a commercial character. It was not a form of economic activity. QED: As neatly as a demonstration in geometry, the conclusion followed that Congress lacked the power in regulating commerce to ban violence against women.

The simplicity of the demonstration does not catch the concern that drove the court, namely, that if the line was not drawn at economic activity, Congress would have the power to regulate every aspect of American life in the guise of regulating commerce. The argument in favor of congressional power to make this law, so the court understood, was that violence motivated by gender deterred women from traveling interstate and from engaging in employment in interstate commerce and conducting businesses in it, and that such violence diminished national productivity, increased medical costs, and decreased trade in interstate products. By aggregating the effect of many such individual gender-related crimes, a substantial impact on interstate commerce was shown. The trouble with this argument for the court was that it went too far.

If this argument were acceptable, the court observed, Congress could enact legislation against ordinary murder and all other crimes of violence. The impact of these crimes on interstate commerce must be even greater than one subset of such crimes, those motivated by gender. Any line between federal criminal law and the police powers of the states would be obliterated.

Teasing out further the implications of the rationale for the legislation, the court observed that the statute itself provided that the statute did not confer federal jurisdiction of any claim for divorce, alimony, distribution of marital property, or child custody. But this limitation seemed to be only a matter of legislative grace. The entire area of domestic relations, taken in the aggregate, had very substantial effects on interstate commerce. Congress could regulate it too, if the argument were accepted that noneconomic activity fell within Congress's power over commerce. Congress as the lawmaker for family relations was a "specter." The specter must be banished by the clearly drawn line between what was commercial and what was not. That line was essential in distinguishing "what is truly national and what is truly local." Now it was the court that evoked the great opinions of John Marshall. *Cohens* was resuscitated. As Marshall had said in dicta there, Congress "has no general right to punish murder" and Congress "cannot punish felonies generally."

The Supreme Court turned to examine Congress's power under section 5 to enforce the guarantees of the fourteenth amendment. Here, there was an equally simple and ample objection. The fourteenth amendment prohibited state action. It did not touch the action of individuals. That had been decided in the early 1880s when the Supreme Court had thrown out the federal indictment of individuals charged with conspiracy in attacking prisoners of the state of Tennessee and lynching one of them. No action by the state had occurred. The conduct of the defendants was beyond the reach of federal power. Therefore, Congress had acted unconstitutionally in 1871 in passing a statute criminalizing the conduct of the Ku Klux Klan and other conspiracies of private individuals formed with one another without the inclusion of state officials. Similarly, in holding sections of the Civil Rights Act of 1875 to be unconstitutional, the Supreme Court had said: "It is State action of a particular character that is prohibited.... [The fourteenth amendment] does not authorize Congress to create a code of municipal law for the regulation of private rights." Accordingly, the Supreme Court had concluded in 1883, Congress could not make individuals liable for denying accommodation at an inn, a restaurant, a theater, or a train because of race.

The court noted the argument that the states were failing to enforce their laws with the corollary that this circumstance distinguished this case from the cases decided in the 1880s where nonaction by the states themselves was not mentioned. But, the court took pains to point out, when Congress had passed the civil rights laws after the Civil War, it had done so because the states were not enforcing their own laws. The situations were parallel. As nonenforcement by the states had not justified the legislation of 1871 and 1875, so nonenforcement today did not justify the Violence Against Women Act.

The court emphasized that the decisions of 1883 deserved particular respect because they had been decided by members of the Supreme Court, all appointed by President Lincoln and his Republican successors, who had "intimate knowledge" of the circumstances in which the fourteenth amendment was adopted. Stressing history, the court did not mention the change in the political attitude toward reconstructing the South after the presidential election of 1876.

Lynching was beyond federal law, racial discrimination in public places and on public transportation was untouchable—these were the judicial precedents that the rule of stare decisis required to be respected. The court also quoted itself in 1991, denying Medicaid patients the right to sue a nursing home regulated by the state of New York: "'Careful adherence to the "state action requirement" preserves an area of individual freedom by limiting the reach of federal law and federal judicial power.'"

Besides the state action requirement, the legislation had to be measured by the criteria of *Boerne*. Neither congruence nor proportion existed between the injury and the remedy provided. If the evil being remedied was the failure of state officials, it was they who should be penalized, but delinquent state officials were not the object of the statute. Brzonkala claimed to have suffered "a brutal assault"—the court's unisex description of the crime alleged. Her remedy, if she was to have one, "must be provided by the Commonwealth of Virginia."

The Supreme Court did not hesitate to make public the terrible thing Brzonkala said Morrison had done to her. What it did stop at publishing was all the language for which the Judicial Committee of Virginia Tech had censured Morrison. "The omitted portions, quoted verbatim in the briefs on file with this Court, consist of boasting, debased remarks about what Morrison would do to women, vulgar remarks that cannot fail to shock and offend." Like the Judicial Committee, the court's sensibility was awake to the coarseness of a common adjective and verb; these were too odious to be in an opinion. Rape and its bureaucratic brush-off were not.

The fault line in the court ran as in the other recent cases. All four dissenters disagreed with the court's analysis of the commerce power of Congress. Congress had assembled a "mountain of data" showing the effect on interstate commerce of violence against women. Years of "the most thorough legislative consideration" had gone into the making of the law. Congress had before it the Department of Justice report on crime, issued in 1988, that three out of four American women would be victims of violent crimes during their lives. Congress had the statement of the surgeon general of the United States in 1992 that violence was the leading cause of injury to women between the ages of fifteen and forty-four. The Bureau of Justice Statistics had showed that since 1974 the assault rate against women had become greater than the assault rate against men. A committee of the American Medical Association in 1991 had reported that 4 million American women each year were battered by their boyfriends or husbands.

As for the protection afforded by the states against such violence, a Senate Report, citing writers on the subject, estimated that arrest rates for domestic assault were as low as 1 percent; that less that 1 percent of all rape victims ever collected damages from their assailants; and that only 4 percent of rapists were actually found guilty of any offense.

The dissent conceded that the methodology of particular studies could be challenged and some of the estimates could be disputed. But that there was sufficient evidence for Congress to act could scarcely be challenged. It was, after all, the function of Congress, not the function of the court, to weigh the evidence for legistation. The *Boerne* criterion, that evil must be demonstrated in the legislative record to the satisfaction of the court, was not disavowed but was implicitly reduced in importance by the dissent.

When Congress in the Civil Rights Act of 1964 had outlawed racial discrimination by hotels, motels, and restaurants in interstate commerce, Congress had acted on anecdotal evidence that individual acts of discrimination cost "thousands to millions of dollars." The legislation had passed muster as constitutional. In enacting the Violence Against Women Act, Congress had evidence that the cost of such violence ranged from $3 billion in 1990 to between $5 billion and $10 billion in 1993. And Congress had evidence that gender-based violence, like race-based discrimination, had the effect of denying its victims full participation in the national economy.

The dissent rejected a firm line between economic and noneconomic activity; indeed, it rejected in general any "categoric" approach. It rejected analysis of this kind for two reasons. First, for the better part of the twentieth century, since 1937, the Supreme Court had accepted the commerce power of Congress as "plenary"; the power had not been restricted to a category. Proper understanding of the power went back to John Marshall's decision in *Gibbons v. Ogden*: "The power, like all others vested in Congress is complete in itself, may be exercised to its utmost extent, and acknowledges no limitations, other than are prescribed in the constitution." The court did not have to accept Congress's word for it, but once the court had found that Congress had a rational basis for its exercise of the commerce power, the court's function was over.

Second, historical examples showed how misguided and how ineffectual had been attempts by the Supreme Court between 1887 and 1937 to create categorical enclaves exempt from the commerce power. These attempts included cases holding that mining was not commerce between the states, that production was not, that manufacturing was not. They included the decisions holding labor relations to be beyond the commerce power. They included the long, sustained, quixotic effort by the court to distinguish between direct and indirect effects on commerce and to hold that only activities "directly" affecting commerce could be regulated by Congress. Some of these categories had set out a sharp, clear concept, only for the concept in the course of time to prove inadequate to measure the interstate impact of industry. Other categories, most notably the apparently bipolar pair, direct—indirect, had proved to be notoriously labile, capable of being manipulated to achieve the result desired on an ad hoc basis. Adherence to the categories had produced the constitutional confrontation with the New Deal and the judicial crisis of 1937. The court now was taking "a step toward recapturing the prior mistakes."

Why was the court embarked on such a mistaken course? The dissent asked the question and answered it. The reason was the court's conviction that there was a "proper sphere of state autonomy." Or, to put it in terms in harmony with the court's other recent cases, it was essential to preserve the fifty sovereigns with legislative work that was their proper domain.

That notion—that federal power must leave an enclave for the states to rule—was attacked by the dissent. Sustaining the Fair Labor Standards Act as it applied generally, the court had said in 1968 that there was "no general doctrine" that the powers of Congress and of the states could not overlap. There were no "inviolable state spheres." As Marshall had written in *Gibbons v. Ogden*, the power of Congress over commerce could be exercised as "absolutely as it would be in a single government."

The country, the dissent noted, was made up of a national government and many state governments. The national power inevitably grew as the national economy grew. In this dynamic world, the interests of the states were not meant to be preserved by the courts, but by politics. A priori definitions of state sovereignty would not serve to limit Congress. It was the structure of the federal government, where representation in Congress was state by state, that set a political limit on what Congress did.

Finally, the dissent noted that the National Association of Attorneys General had supported the Violence Against Women Act. Attorneys general from thirty-eight states had then urged Congress to pass it. When the law was challenged in court, thirty-six attorneys general joined in a brief in its defense. The court was giving the states more autonomy than their own chief prosecutors thought desirable. The irony of championing the autonomy of the state sovereigns when they did not appear to want it was palpable. It was the same ironic result that the court had achieved in *Carter v. Carter Coal*, its last gasp of hostility before capitulating before the New Deal. The dissent noted that Robert Jackson, in *The Struggle for Judicial Supremacy*, had celebrated the irony.

No appeal to history, no sharp reminder of past follies moved the majority. The dissent consoled itself with the observation that not all the cases affirming the extent of the commerce power were now overruled. The new doctrine was not firmly established. Case-by-case, ad hoc review would be necessary to determine what legislation met the new doctrine's test. The situation was unstable and could not last.

The principal dissent did not touch on the section 5 power of Congress. Two of the four dissenters wrote separately to address it. Treating proportionality and congruence as two distinct criteria, these dissenters suggested that the remedy was not disproportionate when it provided damages for conduct, which, "in the main," was already unlawful under state law; and the remedy had congruence in supplementing inadequate state sanctions. But this dissent did not address the text of the fourteenth amendment with its focus on conduct by states, and this dissent concluded abruptly by saying it would not "answer the §5 question."

Two hurdles stood in the way of reliance on section 5. First, state action had to be shown. It could be shown if state inaction was, under the circumstances, the equivalent of state action.

Paradoxically, that should not have been a difficulty. In tort law when one has a duty to act and fails to act, one is liable. Similarly in trust law, if a trustee has a duty to act and fails to act, the trustee is liable for breach of trust. The state university was in the role of guardian of the rights guaranteed Christy Brzonkala by the fourteenth amendment. Failure to defend these rights was the equivalent of action. In special circumstances involving racial discrimination, the Supreme Court had already reached this conclusion. It needed only to make a general rule that a state acted when it shirked its responsibilities.

To make that move would have been a bold development—a development too bold for the dissent and for the majority a retrogression.

In any event, the second hurdle would have remained: The Violence Against Women Act was not directed against a delinquent state but against individuals. Could Congress enforce the guarantees of the fourteenth amendment, when a state defaulted, by making liable the individuals who had escaped sanction by the state? Why could not Congress choose this method of remedying an evil caused by the state default? To uphold the Violence Against Women Act in the particular case of Christy Brzonkala where a state institution could be found to have shielded her attackers would not have had the result, feared by the court, of opening the door to a federal take over of local police functions. But the court, jealous to preserve state jurisdiction, preferred to preserve as well the doctrine of the 1880s that never took state default into account if the suit was against individuals. The lynching and civil rights cases of 1883 had preserved the individual freedom of the members of the Klan and the liberty of racist innkeepers. Incongruously, these were the precedents showing individual liberty was indeed promoted by requiring state action before the fourteenth amendment could be applied.

The case of Christy Brzonkala against Antonio Morrison looked like a case where the state had defaulted on its obligation, but little of the detail of the case appeared in the court's opinion as her complaint was dismissed on jurisdictional grounds without a trial. What resonated at the level of the Supreme Court was not the individual wrong, but echoes of the Marshall court establishing the reach of the commerce power as the commerce of the nation expanded—echoes sounding as the present court repudiated the amplitude of Marshall's interpretation of the power. The case replayed the drama of the post-Reconstruction reaction, the court staying with the analysis that doomed the law against the Klansmen and the attempt to give civil rights beyond the vote to the emancipated people of color. The court rejected the conclusion of Congress and the majority of state attorneys general that federal power was needed to supplement the criminal law of the states with a civil remedy. A sphere was precariously preserved for the fifty sovereigns to police. The middle ground that the national legislature might constitutionally occupy was kept constricted as to section 5 and clipped as to commerce.

CHAPTER 7

Sovereign Remedy

PRESENT DAMAGE, PRESENT DANGER

Alexander Hamilton in *The Federalist* famously wrote that, of the three "departments of power," the judiciary was the "least dangerous to the political rights of the constitution." The judiciary had no army; it had no way of raising taxes; it was dependent on the other branches for the laws it would enforce and for the appointment of its own members. Lacking force, money, and independence in choosing its membership, its capacity to do harm was limited.

Hamilton, aware of aberrations in every government, did not say the judiciary could do no harm, and he underestimated its capabilities. He downplayed the advantage over the other branches that would be given by life tenure, which assured that judges would be in office after presidents and members of Congress were gone. He gave no weight to the advantage a small number of decision makers has, especially if they share a common discipline, over a much larger, far more heterogeneous group that has to respond to a multitude of interests and is dependent on the mobilization of constituencies to pass legislation. If five members of the Supreme Court are in agreement on an agenda, they are mightier than five hundred members of Congress with unmobilized or warring constituencies. A good example is the Intellectual Property Act, proposed as legislation in 1999 to correct *College Savings Bank* with a simple solution. By 2002 the proposed act had not been passed. Similarly, the Religious Liberty Protection Act, first introduced in 1998 in reaction to *Boerne*, had also failed to pass.

Another set of advantages for the judiciary was unnoted by Hamilton. The judiciary has a short line of communication. The justices can speak to each other if they choose, even if often they will prefer memos or e-mail. They do not have to wait for comments from contributors or constituents or columnists. Their secrets are relatively well kept. They are not fodder for the press.

Hamilton, moreover, did not foresee a phenomenon that would occur in modern America. Many persons in a secular society need an authority they can respect and even revere. Law in the abstract may fill this need; a visible institution is even better. Hence, as others have pointed out, Holmes and Brandeis have become secular saints. Hence, there was a sharp sense of disillusionment when the court decided *Bush v. Gore* as if it were a participant in partisan politics at the same time that it, the national court, asserted an authority intruding upon state sovereignty. For two generations the court was the paladin of liberal values, the defender of minorities, the champion of various freedoms—of speech, of the press, of reproductive rights—that put it in the avant-garde of liberal aspirations. The court has enjoyed the prestige and the power conferred by the belief of its admirers.

Possessed of these advantages as it entered battle with Congress, the court is not invulnerable but stronger than Hamilton imagined. The court, Hamilton wrote, has "neither Force nor Will," only judgment. He did not foresee a court with an agenda for restoring power to the several states. Such a court has "Will." As long as the members of the majority remain on the court and stick together on the principal issues of state sovereignty and the criteria for congressional action, the court's position will be difficult to dislodge. In the long run, Hamilton was no doubt right. In our democracy, a small band, entrenched in its position, will ultimately be overwhelmed by the forces arrayed against it. But in the long run we'll all be dead, and much mischief can be done in the short run. The present damage points to the present danger to the exercise of democratic government.

THE RANGE OF POSSIBLE RESPONSE

Congress in its quiver has armaments too heavy or too petty or too awkward to employ. Too heavy is impeachment. Even the legal scholar most convinced that the court is misusing the eleventh amendment and frustrating the fourteenth would quail at the prospect of an impeachment where constitutional interpretations were the issue. At the other end of the spectrum of sanctions, Congress provides the budget of the Supreme Court. Only the salaries of the justices are constitutionally protected from diminution. Salary raises, cheap insurance, accessible parking, law clerks, secretaries, and marshals have to be budgeted. A mean-spirited Congress, bent on reprisal, could cripple or curtail the court in a variety of budgetary ways. Picayune revenge of this kind is beneath the dignity of the national legislature.

The Senate does have the power to confirm nominations to the Supreme Court. The Judiciary Committee can gain some idea of a nominee's approach to constitutional questions. But it is hard to gather from a nominee more than generalities bordering on platitudes, difficult to predict the precise form an issue will take, and improper for the Senate to secure a commitment as to how a nominee will vote on a given matter. The executive branch probably has greater flexibility in informally informing itself about a prospective nominee's likely approach, but it, too, would act improperly in attempting to bind a future justice's vote. Control of the court through the process of nomination and confirmation cannot occur without hitches, uncertainties, improprieties, and surprises.

The remedy most readily available to Congress is legislation drafted after careful study of the opinions of the Supreme Court establishing the constitutional criteria and, if possible, using powers not constrained by the court. The proposed Intellectual Property Act, for example, employs the power over patents and copyrights that article I grants to Congress. Exercising that plenary power, the bill excludes from the class of possible patentees any state not waiving its own immunity from infringement suits. No decision of the Supreme Court denies the existence in Congress of the patent power, no decision denies the right of Congress to exercise it conditionally. If proportionality were to be required in the exercise of an article I power, the proportion appears fair. The state must do unto others what it would have others do unto it.

Another power that the Supreme Court has not denied is the power of Congress to direct the spending of federal funds and to condition federal funding on the states meeting the conditions set by Congress. In this way Congress has forced the states to set speed limits on the highways in order to secure federal highway funds. To obtain federal funds for education, it should be possible for Congress to require the states not to discriminate on the basis of age or disability in hiring or firing faculty or staff.

Whether Congress could attach to a grant a condition unrelated to the purpose of a grant is not clear. If the spending power is viewed as totally within the domain of the legislature, there should be no restriction on the power. A Supreme Court that was determined to defend state sovereignty might, nonetheless, attempt to distinguish the germane from the ungermane condition, voiding the latter.

A third approach for Congress is to do piecemeal what it had attempted to do wholesale. In an attempt to salvage RFRA after *Boerne*, the Religious Liberty Protection Act was introduced into Congress. "Mindful of the limitations enunciated by the Court in *Boerne*" on Congress's fourteenth amendment powers, some members of Congress favored an approach that would "employ" all . . . remaining avenues of established Congressional authority." A less ambitious approach that succeeded in the enactment of legislation combined two incongruous areas of governmental power to impose the RFRA requirements only as to regulations governing the use of land and as to the treatment of the religion of prisoners and others confined in institutions. It cannot be assumed that the new law will pass the criteria of *Boerne*.

Legislation, it appears, can likely extend protection against the states to patentees and copyright holders and to employees of state institutions receiving federal funding. It is not certain that other state employees can be assured the protection of federal antidiscrimination statutes. The fate of the Religious Land Use and Institutionalized Persons Act is unpredictable. Trademark holders have no clear remedy. The Violence Against Women Act cannot be resuscitated unless the constitution is amended or the members of the majority change.

Amendment of the constitution is a remedy but such a gargantuan undertaking that it is unlikely to be attempted and very unlikely to succeed.

THE SOVEREIGN REMEDY

The sovereign remedy for ills in a democracy is exploration and exposition of a problem, leaving it to the good sense of those who can effect its solution to take the necessary steps.

It is the duty of lawyers, the Model Code of Professional Responsibility teaches, to work for the reform of the law. It is their duty because lawyers best know its imperfections. Lawyers do not cease to have this duty when they become judges. It is the right of judges, the Code of Judicial Conduct proclaims, to speak and write for the improvement of the law. Judges, even more than lawyers, will know and feel its imperfections. What reform or improvement is more evidently needed than light on decisions that fail to carry out purposes set out by the constitution itself?

The failure arises, in the first instance, from the Supreme Court's lack of self-consciousness. The court has conceived itself as a neutral umpire above the fray. It does not think of itself as a player. It does not look at itself as an entity wielding the nation's power. It identifies with the constitution itself. Identification of this sort confers upon it invisibility to itself.

Abstractness accompanies this invisibility. The court's decisions here are driven by abstractions. A mind-set, not uncommon in judges, rejoices in rules because rules appear to provide certainties. Recitation of the rules boxes the facts into established categories. The expenditure of energy in thought is reduced.

Facts are unruly. Facts should drive cases. That is the experience of most trial judges and of many appellate judges. Let me state the facts, experienced counsel may say, the law will follow. The facts have the function of bringing the judges as close as possible to the gritty tangles and unexpected turns that run through human situations. At the center of the facts are the persons who brought the facts into existence or responded to them. Forget the facts, and you forget the persons helped or hurt by the decisions.

For the Supreme Court, proceeding as it appears to proceed in these cases with an agenda, the facts are of minor importance and the persons affected are worthy of almost no attention. The court is focused on the large questions of constitutional law and on grand conceptions, such as sovereignty. The people and their problems that have been grist for the constitutional mill are incidental. So it was of no particular interest to this court that the bulk of St. Peter's Church in Boerne may not have fallen within the historic district, or that Roberts's patent for a set of algorithms may have had little chance of surviving litigation. The court wanted to decide these cases on the big issues. All the facts surrounding the assault on Christy Brzonkala and the lack of effective response by state officials were also a matter of indifference to the court focused on the precedents interpreting the fourteenth amendment. That these facts illustrated the sort of denial of protection that Congress had addressed was beside the point.

Almost complete indifference to the individual plaintiffs has been accompanied in these cases by an absence of interest in the number of persons negatively affected by the court's rulings. The plaintiffs, rightly of significance in themselves, were also surrogates for wider groups whose cause was lost with theirs. The grand course of great constitutional litigation decides a case and affects a continent, it acts upon the issues presented and sets precedent for a century. The rightness or wrongness of the decision, so the court assumes, cannot be determined by counting the people who may suffer.

Much may be said for this methodological assumption. There is no good way of measuring all the waves that flow from a decision or calculating all the unanticipated consequences. When the court, however, has adopted a methodology that seeks to quantify the evil Congress is seeking to remedy, it is indefensible to ignore the size of the protected class. If, for example, only 1 percent of the 4.5 million state employees should annually suffer an act of discrimination by a state employer, that would be forty-five thousand persons, surely not a negligible number. If only 1 percent of women were each year denied effective protection against gender-motivated crime, that would be 1.3 million women. The numbers become small only when the court counts only the incidents described in congressional reports.

This observation leads from the abstractness of the Supreme Court's approach, no doubt nothing new, to what is both new and destructive in its approach to federal legislation. To strike down a law as incongruous or as disproportionate or as both is an invention of *Boerne*.

The invention is an invasion of the legislature. What legislators do is to make laws they think fit the situations they have heard about. They form their ideas of congruence and proportion, as most people do, intuitively. They do so because there is no other guide.

Nothing in the experience of justices of the Supreme Court, nothing in the constitutional role of that court, provides the court with a measure. For the members of the court, as much as for the members of Congress, it's just a hunch as to what seems reasonable. No defensible theory of the constitution justifies the justices preferring their hunch to the work of the legislators. Judicial restraint is abandoned when they do.

Dante's *Divine Comedy* is commonly regarded as a classic of Western literature, not only for its beauty of expression but for the depth of its allegorical treatment of human sin. In its Purgatorio the proud are crushed beneath rocks, the envious have their eyes sewed shut, and the lustful are burned by fire. Are these purgations proportionate to, and congruous with, the faults they punish? Some would say yes, others no, many would be unsure. If a supreme poet cannot convince us of what is a proportionate and congruent remedy for specific evils, a supreme court cannot do better. The court's pronouncements are ipse dixits carrying no conviction. A fortiori, that is the case when the court's pronouncement of proportionality is demonstrably wrong, as when the remedy for patent infringement by a state was said to be disproportionate to the evil addressed, even though the only patent suits against a state that would prevail would be ones where the state was in fact an infringer.

The criteria of proportionality and congruence have been linked by the court with the requirement of a record, made by Congress, that the court will scrutinize. This invention was indispensable once the two criteria were announced. There had to be in existence something that the court could identify, where the evil being remedied was described. By habit, as it were, the court found something resembling a report and recommendations made by a federal administrative agency, accompanied by the record of a hearing, in the reports and recommendations of congressional committees and the records made before them. In determining what Congress has relied on, the court has chiefly looked at these documents, while also occasionally referring to speeches in Congress.

The institution of judicial review of a legislative record is a particularly bold way of exercising supremacy over Congress, or, to put it another way, of the court itself playing a legislative part. Inevitably, in such a review, some pieces of the record before Congress will strike some members of the court more forcefully than the same pieces of evidence will strike other members of the court. What is more natural? The justices are all acting as legislators, exercising their own good judgment as to what is probative and what is irrelevant and so making up their own minds as to whether the legislation that was passed should have been passed.

In this process of legislative discernment the value judgments of the justices naturally play a predominant part. What, in the eyes of the minority, are thousands of examples of discrimination by the states against the disabled are reduced, in the eyes of the majority, to a handful of anecdotes—reduced not only in gross number but in persuasiveness because the majority notes that most of the allegations of most of the cases have not been tested by litigation.

In this treatment of the evidence before Congress another test is implied and used: Anecdotes don't count. Anecdotes don't count? How have legislators over the centuries worked? Stories they have heard, stories of their own lives, stories of family, friends, constituents have been the stuff of legislative intelligence. To be sure in modern times, statistical reports have had a role, but not so much so that they are a sine qua non.

How did the court get itself in this awkward posture of monitoring Congress the way appellate courts monitor administrative agencies? The criteria were invented as a way of determining whether Congress had overstepped the role the court had assigned it under the fourteenth amendment. That role being remedial, the court gave itself the task of determining whether the legislation was truly remedial.

The preventative could be encompassed by the remedial. At times the court has said as much. In applying its criteria, however, the court has demanded that Congress provide examples of evils that have actually occurred. "Remedial" has been construed narrowly. That Congress could be possessed of foresight has not been given credit by the court.

A larger question is why Congress should be confined to the remedial. The fourteenth amendment assigns Congress the role of enforcing its guarantees. The amendment assigns no role to the court. In normal English, the power to enforce carries with it a limited discretion to be exercised by the enforcer as to what is being enforced. A teacher in a classroom does not make up the school's disciplinary rules but in enforcing them has some discretion as to whether a rule against disrupting a classroom includes saying who has the burden of proof when the teacher hears someone throwing an eraser behind the teacher's back. Enforcement of the fourteenth amendment's guarantee of liberty, one might well think, depends on an equally discretionary judgment as to whether the individual or the state has the burden of proof when an individual points to an infringement. But the Supreme Court has swept even such a procedural determination within its broad assertion of its sole competence to say what the constitution means.

Why, in the last analysis, is the court's competence sole? Citizens sometimes have to have a sense of their constitutional rights. Every official in the country, from the president down, has some sense of what the constitution means in order to perform the duties of office. Congress enacts legislation with the expectation that it is acting within the constitution. The president signs only what he is advised is constitutional. Surely the coordinate branches of government deserve more than a nod in their direction before their understanding of the constitution is stamped as illegitimate. Especially when the Supreme Court itself is divided five to four, or when, as happened in *Boerne*, a new rule is proposed to replace an old rule followed by the court itself, one would suppose that the combined judgment of Congress and the president might be persuasive. If not as a strict requirement of law, but as a matter of prudence, the court might reasonably be expected to go to lengths to avoid branding the old rule as unconstitutional, thereby rejecting the reasoning of other branches of government and its own precedents. The three branches were designed as a cooperative enterprise. Supremacy over the courts was not designed as supremacy over the country.

In the design of our government only the people are supreme; and the people have exercised their power by creating a constitution granting legislative power over defined subjects to Congress and vesting executive power in the president and judicial power in the judiciary. No one of these delegated powers is sovereign over the others; none is sovereign in the sense of being the supreme repository of power.

The states appear in the original constitution as determining the electors for the House of Representatives; as the units determining the number of representatives; as units guaranteed two senators apiece, chosen by the state's legislature; as units choosing the electors of the president; as units appointing officers of the state militia; as the owners of territory that may be ceded or sold to the United States; as units that may permit the importation of slaves up to 1808; as litigants in certain kinds of cases in the federal courts; as having their public acts, records, and judicial proceedings entitled to full faith and credit by the other states; as conferring privileges and immunities on their citizens, entitling them to the same in the other states; as bound to return fugitives from justice or from slavery to the state from which the fugitive has escaped; as immune from division or merger except by consent of their legislatures; as callers of constitutional conventions; and as ratifiers of constitutional amendments. By amendment of the constitution, the powers not delegated by the constitution to the United States or prohibited to the states are reserved to the respective states or to the people. The judicial power of the United States does not extend to suits against a state by citizens of another state or of a foreign state. Voting in the House of Representatives, in the case where a presidential election goes to the House, is to be by state delegation, each state having one vote. Election by senators is now to be by popular vote in each state. A state can regulate or ban the transportation or importation of liquor within its borders.

The states are expressly forbidden to make treaties; grant letters of marque; coin money; emit bills of credit; make anything but gold or silver legal tender for debts; pass any bill of attainder; pass an ex post facto law; impair the obligation of contracts; grant a title of nobility; or, without the consent of Congress, lay duties on any import or export or tonnage; or keep troops or warships; or make a compact with any other state; or engage in war. The president may call to service the militia of the several states. The constitution and the laws made under it shall be the supreme law of the land, "and the Judges in every State shall be bound thereby, any Thing in the Constitution or Laws of any State to the Contrary."

Twenty times in the constitution as amended, the states appear. Sometimes they are given powers, sometimes they are subjected to prohibitions. Their vital place is assured by their role in elections—the election of members of Congress and the election of the president, while their relative equality is preserved by the assignment of two senators to each state and the requirement of voting by states, each counted as one, when the presidential election falls to the House. The tenth amendment reserves powers to them as well as to the people. Nowhere in the entire document are the states identified as sovereigns.

The claim that the sovereignty of the states is constitutional rests on an audacious addition to the eleventh amendment, a pretense that it incorporates the idea of state sovereignty. Neither the text nor the legislative history of the amendment supports this claim, nor does an appeal to the history contemporaneous with the amendment. A rhetorical advantage is gained by the current court referring to state sovereignty as "an eleventh amendment" matter. The constitutional connection is imaginary.

Sovereignty in the classic sense was indivisible. Apparently such a concept of the sovereign was in Holmes's mind when he asserted that one cannot sue a sovereign because that would put a sovereign above the sovereign. But not one of the fifty states, nor the United States itself, is such a sovereign. Authority is divided between the states and the nation, and again among the three branches of the government. Sovereignty cannot be found in America in the form classically imagined. It is not directly or indirectly ascribed to the states by the constitution of the United States.

The immunity of the sovereign monarch from suit was a principle of English common law. It was a principle accepted by the federal government and by several states of the Union. Like other common law principles, it is open to being overridden by federal law and by the federal constitution. In a variety of ways, most notably in federal habeas corpus proceedings, in the review of state court judgments by the Supreme Court of the United States, and in suits against state officers fictionally treated as individuals, the sovereignty of the states has been disregarded in American legal practice. As federal law is the supreme law of the land, at no time in the history of the United States has sovereignty of the states been intact. The sovereign immunity of the states is explicitly denied by article III of the constitution setting out the cases in which the states must answer in federal litigation.

As sovereign immunity of the states from suit does not appear in the constitution, where does it come from in the United States? It is judge-made, first as a common law doctrine, later as a doctrine of constitutional law. Is there a basis on which the judge-made constitutional rule can be defended?

The strongest argument in its support is the so-called structural one—that, to preserve the structure of a federal union, to keep it from collapsing into a single unitary system, the states must be immune from private lawsuits. The outline of an argument is offered, but no demonstration follows. It is conceded by its proponents that the United States itself can sue any state in order to enforce an applicable law of the United States. The concession admits that the states are subordinate. The fourteenth amendment expressly subjects the states to prohibitions, with whose enforcement Congress is charged. State sovereignty becomes a ghost. The alleged immunity from suit does nothing to restore the powers the states are forbidden to exercise or to eliminate the subordination to which the constitution subjects them. What is the point of supposing there is a structural necessity for something that has already been removed?

A second, and old, argument for state sovereign immunity is the need to preserve the states' solvency. The argument had some force after the Revolution and after the Civil War and Reconstruction. It has no force now, when a state invoking immunity would destroy its credit rather than salvage it. It makes no sense now when cities, like New York City, with budgets far larger than that of many states, have risked bankruptcy without fatal harm to their governance. It is an argument without a supporter among the states, all of which want to participate in the market for government securities without an asterisk saying, "These borrowers cannot be held accountable."

Still, it may be argued, the states do value their immunity in tort, and this immunity keeps taxpayers' dollars from being drained by unjustified lawsuits. But the lawsuits may be for real injuries committed by a state. Most fundamentally, why should a state tortfeasor not pay compensation for the injury it inflicts?

The final argument for immunity is that the dignity of the state demands it. A moral quality appears to be attributed to the state that is inexplicable unless the state is taken to be the replacement of the prince. Persons do have dignity. The defenders of state immunity have proclaimed that states are not persons. Whence is their dignity? Is the term not tautological?

Not in the constitution, not implied by the structure of the constitution, not needed for solvency, not explained by dignity, the immunity of the fifty states is a relic of the past without justification of any kind today. It is revolting, as Holmes wrote, that a legal doctrine have no better reason for its current existence than that so it was laid down in the time of Henry IV.

Not only is the doctrine unjustified, it presents the most serious difficulties in its employment. First, the immunity of the states has, as it were, metastasized. Immunity would be strange enough if confined to the governors of the fifty states or to their core political officers. It is a fantastic doctrine when extended to what are, by unthinking metaphor, arms of the sovereigns. No human being has multiple arms. Like the heads of a hydra or the legs of a centipede, these appendages are multiple. The very uncertainty of where the line will be drawn by a court extends the penumbra of immunity beyond the most obvious. Certainly in-

cluded are the state universities and their presses, their research
laboratories, their stadiums, and their campus stores. Probably
included are all the colleges substantially supported by the
states, even though their status is not shown by their names, like
the City College of New York. Certainly included are all state
hospitals, and all state schools for the blind, the deaf, and the
mentally disabled. These entities may be engaged in commercial
activities, such as licensing patents or selling insurance, football
tickets, sporting equipment, or books. They may be engaged in
the production of fiction, such as *The Last of the Menu Girls*.
They are nonetheless covered by the mantle of the sovereign.
The parade of sovereigns before the Supreme Court includes a
marketer of insurance, Florida Prepaid; an ethnic press, Arte
Publico Press; a small educational institution, the University of
Montevallo. In reality, then, there are not fifty sovereigns in
America, but at least two thousand entitled to claim the dignity
and protection that accompany the title.

Why is this metastasis tolerated? None of the asserted reasons has the slightest connection to this extended sovereignty.

A second difficulty: Sovereign immunity from suit cannot be
extended across the board without intolerable injury to the enforcement of federal standards nor can it be curtailed without
logical contradiction. *Ex parte Young* offers a solution that is indefensible: the acts of an officer of the state may be enjoined by
a single federal judge if these acts offend the fourteenth amendment, so that at one and the same time the individual officer's
acts are treated as state action and as nonstate action. The self-
contradictory compromise continues only because of the doc-
trinaire belief that in such cases of unconstitutional action, the
states cannot be named as the defendants. In its most sovereign-

like activity of executing criminals, a state must submit to the fiction that not the state but the warden is prevented from acting when the writ of habeas corpus is issued by the federal judge.

A doctrine that has swelled beyond bounds, a doctrine that cannot be consistently applied or reconciled with the federal system, state immunity from suit suffers from one further, final difficulty for a doctrine of the law. It is unjust. Why should a state not pay its just debts, why should it be saved from compensating for the harm it tortiously causes? Why should it be subject to federal patent law, federal copyright law, and federal prohibitions of discrimination in employment and not be accountable for the patent or copyright it invades, not accountable for its discriminatory acts as an employer? No reason in the constitution or in the nature of things or in the acts of Congress supplies an answer. The states are permitted to act unjustly only because the highest court in the land has, by its own will, moved the middle ground and narrowed the nation's power.

NOTES

PROLOGUE: A RECURRENT
STRUGGLE IS RESUMED

the copyright case: infra, chapter 4; **the age discrimination case:** infra, chapter 5; **the woman raped by members of the football team:** infra, chapter 6.

"[T]he States entered the federal system with their sovereignty intact": *Blatchford v. Native Village of Noatak*, 501 U.S. 775, 779 (1991); quoted in *Seminole Tribe of Florida v. Florida*, 517 U.S. 44, 150 (1996) and in *Alden v. Maine*, 527 U.S. 706, 713 (1999).

"neither a national nor a federal Constitution": James Madison, Number 39, *The Federalist*.

These express powers were construed...under John Marshall: *McCulloch v. Maryland*, 17 U.S. (4 Wheat.) 316 (1819).

The standards apply to the states, but...cannot be enforced: *infra*, chapters 4 and 5.

"There must be congruence and proportionality": *City of Boerne v. Flores*, 521 U.S. 507, 520 (1997).

"widespread and persisting deprivation of constitutional rights": id. at 526.

"anecdotal evidence": id. at 531 and *Bd. of Trustees of the Univ. of Alabama v. Garrett*, 121 S. Ct. 955, 966 (2001); see infra, chapter 5.

The Violence Against Women Act held unconstitutional: infra, chapter 6.

The recurrent battle: Robert H. Jackson, *The Struggle for Judicial Supremacy* (New York: Alfred A. Knopf, 1941), xii–xvii.

the institution has more influence on individuals: id., vii.

"ahistorical literalism": *Alden v. Maine*, 527 U.S. 706, 730 (1999).

a contradiction sits at the center: See infra, chapter 3.

Dred Scott v. Sandford: 60 U.S. 393 (19 How.) (1857); *Lochner v. New York*: 198 U.S. 45 (1905); *Carter v. Carter Coal Company*, 298 U.S. 238 (1936).

CHAPTER I

THE BATTLE OF BOERNE

A unique contribution: See John T. Noonan Jr., *The Lustre of Our Country: The American Experience of Religious Freedom* (Berkeley: University of California Press, 1998), 75–91 (hereafter *Lustre*).

The mother country: id. at 57–58.

A would-be imitator: id. at 267–275.

the umpire of the experiment: id. at 91.

The states had no intention: id. at 96.

New Hampshire even had a provision: New Hampshire Constitution, pt. 2 (1784), in James Fairbanks Colby, comp., *Manual of the Constitution of the State of New Hampshire* (Manchester: J. B. Clarke, 1912), 110–113; *Lustre* at 99.

A foreign observer like Tocqueville: *Lustre* at 95.

Most important, religion was exercised freely: id. at 119–137.

The Supreme Court's one sustained venture: id., 252–254; **Supreme Court upheld**: *Reynolds v. United States*, 98 U.S. 145 (1878); **federal statute:** An Act to punish and prevent the Practice of Polygamy in the Territories of the United States and other Places, and disapproving and annulling certain Acts of the Legislative Assembly of the Territory of Utah, 12 Stat. 501–502 (July 1, 1862); **court also upheld a territorial statute:** *Murphy v. Ramsey*, 114 U.S. 15 (1885); **court enforced a federal law confiscating the property:** *The Late Corporation of the Church of Jesus Christ of Latter Day Saints v. United States*, 140 U.S. 665 (1891).

various state prosecutions: See e.g., *Nicholls v. Mayor and Sch. Comm. of Lynn*, 297 Mass. 65, 7 N.E. 577 (1937) (expulsion from school); **When the Witnesses appealed to the Supreme Court:** *Lustre* at 241–242.

The Supreme Court decided that religious liberty: *Cantwell v. Connecticut*, 310 U.S. 296 (1940).

The makers of the fourteenth amendment did have a sense that the religious freedom of the newly emancipated slaves: Kurt T. Lash, "The Second Adoption of the Free Exercise Clause: Religious Exemptions under the Fourteenth Amendment." 88 *Nw. U.L.R.* 1106, 1134–1135 (1994).

Three overlapping reasons: Freedom of speech and freedom of the press read into fourteenth amendment: *Gitlow v. New York*, 286 U.S. 652, 666 (1925); **withdrawn from the business of invalidating governmental regulation:** *West Coast Hotel v. Parrish*, 300 U.S. 379 (1937); **"in the delusion of racial or religious conceit":** *Cantwell*, 310 U.S. 296 at 310.

Writing for the court, Felix Frankfurter: *Minersville School District v. Gobitis*, 310 U.S. 586 (1940); **"an interest inferior to none":** id. at 595.

"If there is any fixed star": *West Virginia State Board of Education v. Barnette*, 319 U.S. 624, 642 (1943).

"Providing public schools ranks at the very apex": *Wisconsin v. Yoder*, 406 U.S. 205, 213 (1972); **"[B]elief and action cannot be neatly confined"**: id. at 220; **"[A] regulation neutral on its face"**: id. at 220.

The national government was always found to have had a national interest: See e.g., *Bowen v. Roy*, 476 U.S. 693 (1986); *Goldman v. Weinberger*, 475 U.S. 503 (1986); *United States v. Lee*, 455 U.S. 252 (1983).

The governmental interest... had to be "compelling": See *Employment Div. v. Smith*, 494 U.S. 872, 894–895 (1990) (concurrence, collecting cases)

"Compelling interest"... could be dispensed with: *Lyng v. Northwest Indian Cemetery Protective Assn.*, 485 U.S. 439, 447 (1998); **"the Indians' ability to practice"**: id. at 451.

It would not have been a stretch to hold that Oregon had a compelling interest: *Employment Div.*, 494 U.S. 872 at 905 (concurrence).

It did so without even asking: Michael W. McConnell, "Free Exercise Revisionism and the *Smith* Decision," 57 *U. Chi. L. Rev.* 1109, 1113 (1990).

To achieve this result, the court had to put a new skin: *Employment Div. v. Smith*, 494 U.S. 872 (1990) (opinion by Scalia, J., joined by Rehnquist, C.J., and by White, Stevens, and Kennedy, JJ.); ***Cantwell*** **and *Yoder* explained**: id. at 881; **a Mormon case**: *Reynolds v. United States*, 98 U.S. 145 (1879), twice cited in *Employment Div.* at 879 and 885; **"Instead the opinion of Justice Frankfurter"**: id. at 879.

"sweeping result,"... "disregard our consistent application of free exercise doctrine": id. at 892 (O'Connor, J., joined by Brennan,

Marshall, and Blackmun, JJ.); **The misreading of *Cantwell* and of *Yoder*:** id. at 896.

A formidable and unusual coalition: See Gustav Niebuhr, *Disparate Groups United Behind Civil Rights Bill on Religious Freedom, Washington Post*, October 16, 1993 at 7, available at 1994 WL 2093750 (noting "no fewer than 48 religious and civil liberties groups" from People for the American Way and the ACLU to the National Association of Evangelicals, the U.S. Conference of Catholic Bishops, and major Jewish organizations).

Incredibly . . . free exercise was being characterized as a luxury: Testimony of John H. Buchanan, Jr., chairman, People for the American Way Action Fund, Religious Freedom Restoration Act of 1990: Hearings on H.R. 5377 before the House Committee on the Judiciary, 102d Cong. at 53 (1990); **"The Dred Scott of first amendment law":** Testimony of Nadine Strossen, president of the American Civil Liberties Union, Religious Freedom Act of 1992: Hearings on S. 2969 before the Senate Judiciary Committee, 102d Cong. at 171 (1992). See also Statement of Elder Dallin H. Oaks in the same hearings, p. 33 (1992); Testimony of Robert P. Dugan Jr., Religious Freedom Restoration Act of 1991: Hearings on H.R. 2797 before the House Committee on the Judiciary, 102d Cong. at 13 (1992).

RFRA: 42 U.S.C. §2000bb; **House and Senate votes on RFRA:** 139 *Cong. Rec.* 26416 (103rd Cong., 1st sess., October 27, 1993); 139 *Cong. Rec.* 27241 (103rd Cong., 1st sess., November 3, 1993).

"self-executing": *City of Boerne v. Flores*, 521 U.S. 507, 522 (1997).

The Congress that drafted the fourteenth amendment: Joseph T. Sneed III, *Footprints on the Rocks of the Mountain: An Account of the Enactment of the Fourteenth Amendment* (West Coast Print Center, 1997), 330–331, 370; Stephen A. Engel, "The *McCulloch* Theory of the Fourteenth Amendment: *City of Boerne v. Flores* and the Original

Understanding of Section 5," 109 *Yale L.J.* 115, 131–134 (1997); *Cong. Globe*, 29th Cong., 1st sess. (1866): 43, 2765.

Dred Scott: *Scott v. Sandford*, 60 U.S. (19 How.) 393 (1857).

"It is the power of Congress which has been enlarged": *Ex parte Virginia*, 100 U.S. 339, 345–346 (1879).

"Let the end be legitimate": *McCulloch v. Maryland*, 17 U.S. (4 Wheat.) 316, 421 (1819).

the court had held that a test of literacy . . . did not violate the fourteenth amendment: *Lassiter v. Northampton County Bd. of Elections*, 360 U.S. 45 (1959); **Congress had responded:** see Voting Rights Act of 1965 41(a), 42 U.S.C. §1971(a)(2)(C) (banning literacy tests).

The evidence that Congress was remedying: *Katzenbach v. Morgan*, 384 U.S. 641, 654 n.14 (1966).

The history of St. Peter's: "St. Peter the Apostle Catholic Church," http//www.massintransit.com/tx/stpeter-tx-boerne/index.html, accessed July 18, 2001.

The early stages of the battle of Boerne: *San Antonio Express News*, August 8, 1993; **"like sardines":** id.; **over $600,000 in pledges:** id.; **historical value of church:** James Steely to Anna Marie Davison, June 23, 1992; **The archbishop and then the pope:** Thomas P. Sullivan to Archbishop Flores, June 1993; **petition to the pope:** reprinted, *Boerne Star*, October 13, 1993; **question as to extent of historic zone:** *San Antonio Express*, January 30, 1996; **actions of landmarks commission and city council:** *Boerne Star*, April 20, 1994; **"morally and grossly unjust":** *Hill County Recorder*, April 5, 1995; **move to Rainbow Senior Center:** id.

The case in the district court: *Flores v. City of Boerne*, 877 F. Supp. 355 (M.D. Texas, 1995); **the case in the Fifth Circuit:** *Flores v. City of Boerne*, 73 F.3d 1352 (5th Cir. 1996), *cert. granted*, 519 U.S. 926 (1996). Almost in parallel with *Boerne* a case arose in the Ninth

Circuit in which RFRA was invoked. In Eugene, Oregon, a young man was arrested on strong suspicion that he had murdered three teenagers. As he awaited trial, he asked that a priest hear his confession. The confession was made by means of an intercom and routinely recorded as a matter of prison policy. The district attorney subpoenaed the recording to introduce at the man's trial. No Oregon law forbade such evidence, and no Oregon judge would prevent its introduction. Invoking RFRA, the priest and his archbishop asked the federal court to protect the secrecy of the religious rite that had been engaged in. The district attorney argued that RFRA was unconstitutional. Like the Fifth Circuit, the Ninth Circuit held RFRA to be in accord with precedent. It ruled that RFRA forbade the secular intrusion into a sacrament—a new, startling, and unlawful aggression against free exercise. *Mockaitis v. Harcleroad*, 104 F.3d 1522 (9th Cir. 1997) (per Noonan, J., joined by Thompson and Kleinfeld, JJ.).

"not easy to discern": *City of Boerne*, 521 U.S. 507 at 519; "must have wide latitude": id. at 520; *"the distinction exists"*: id.

"There must be a congruence and proportionality": id. (opinion by Kennedy, J. with Rehnquist, C.J., and Stevens, Scalia, Thomas, and Ginsburg, JJ., concurring). For a searching critique of *Boerne*, see Evan H. Caminker, "'Appropriate' Means–Ends constraints on Section 5 Powers," 53 *Stan. L. Rev.* 1127–1199 (2001).

"imposition of subjective judgment": *Hamelin v. Michigan*, 501 U.S. 957, 985 (1991) (Scalia, J., joined by Rehnquist, C.J.).

"anecdotal evidence": *City of Boerne*, 521 U.S. 507 at 531; "adverse effects": id.; "in the past 40 years": id. at 530; *"sweeping coverage"*: id. at 532.

exemption as establishment: id. at 536–537 (Stevens, J., concurring)

exemptions already accepted by the court: See Selective Draft Act §4, 40 Stat. 76, 79 (May 18, 1917); Selective Training and Service

Act of 1940 §5(g), 54 Stat. 885, 889 (September 16, 1940) (draft exemptions); Volstead Act §3, 41 Stat. 305, 308–309 (October 28, 1919); 26 U.S.C. §3127 (Social Security exemption); 10 U.S.C. §744 (exception for religious apparel); 102 Stat. 1826 (1988) (suspension of funds for logging road). See generally, *Lustre*, at 222–226.

One ... dissenters explicitly agreed: *City of Boerne*, 521 U.S. 507 at 544 (O'Connor, J.).

"Who's in charge?": *San Antonio Express*, June 27, 1997; **compromise:** *San Antonio Express*, September 26, 2000.

CHAPTER 2

SUPERIOR BEINGS

Samuel Simple, his law clerks, and his friends: These persons have already conducted a discussion of *Boerne* and RFRA in "The Pilgrim's Process," chapter 7 of my book, *The Lustre of our Country: The American Experience of Religious Freedom* (Berkeley: University of California Press, 1997), 179–210. Familiar with their different perspectives, I return to them to explore a basic building block in the Supreme Court's new approach.

concept of immunity not prominent when Simple went to school in the 1960s: When in 1975 Gerald Gunther, a leading authority on constitutional law, completed the ninth edition of *Constitutional Law: Cases and Materials,* neither the eleventh amendment nor sovereign immunity appeared in the book's index, as they had not in the preceding editions dating back to 1937. The subjects were similarly absent from the 1996 casebook on constitutional law, dating back to 1964, edited by five prominent scholars—William B. Lockhart, Yale Kamisar, Jesse H. Choper, Steven H. Shiffrin, and Richard H. Fallon, Jr. In the field of constitutional law, crowded by issues of intense debate, the eleventh amendment and sovereign immunity did not loom large. Much has changed since 1964.

The novelty of the Supreme Court's approach is wittily captured by Seth P. Waxman, who, as solicitor general of the United States, lost six federalism cases in 1999 and 2000. He invokes the beginning of the Stanley Kubrick film *2001*, in which a bunch of apes are standing in a forest. "They're astounded to see a huge black stone monolith in their midst. They don't know what to make of it. They wander around it, they grunt at it, they bang on it. But they don't know where it came from, and they don't know what it means." Waxman goes on: "I know the feeling. And so do so many of my colleagues who grew up in the law at a time when the Eleventh Amendment was understood to mean more or less what it said." Waxman, "Foreward: Does the Solicitor General Matter?" 53 *Stan. L. Rev.* 1115 (2001).

"burden on the states": *City of Boerne v. Flores*, 521 U.S. 507, 534 (1997); see supra, chapter 1.

a sovereign cannot be sued by an individual: *Hans v. Louisiana*, 134 U.S. 1 (1890); **by an Indian tribe:** *Blatchford v. Noatak Village*, 501 U.S. 775 (1991) (Scalia, J., joined by Rehnquist, C.J., and White, Blackmun, O'Connor, Kennedy, and Souter, JJ.); **by a foreign government:** *Monaco v. Mississippi*, 292 U.S. 313 (1934); **and even though Congress exercised its article I powers:** *Seminole Tribe of Florida v. Florida*, 517 U.S. 44 (1996).

"central to sovereign dignity": *Alden v. Maine*, 527 U.S. 706, 715 (1998).

"Even where the Constitution vests in Congress complete lawmaking authority": *Seminole Tribe*, 517 U.S. 44 at 72 (Rehnquist, C.J., joined by O'Connor, Kennedy, Scalia, and Thomas, JJ.).

"inherent" or "implicit": *Alden*, 527 U.S. 708, 730 (citing *Blatchford*, 501 U.S. 775 at 781).

habeas corpus petitions of prisoners: e.g., *DePetris v. Kuykendall*, 239 F.3d 1057 (9th Cir. 2001); *Dorsey v. Chapman*, 262 F.3d 1181 (11th

Cir. 2001); **habeas corpus stay of execution:** e.g., *Harris v. Vasquez*, 901 F.2d 724 (9th Cir. 1990).

"stripped": *Ex parte Young*, 209 U.S. 123, 160 (1908); **facts:** id., 127–141.

Moby Dick: See e.g., *Strahan v. Cox*, 939 F. Supp. 963 (D. Mass. 1996) (injunction against Massachusetts officials on behalf of endangered whales). The court rejected the argument that *Seminole Tribe* should lead to state immunity from the Endangered Species Act. The Supreme Court has not decided the issue. See Note, "An Inapt Fiction: The Use of the *Ex Parte Young* Doctrine for Environmental Citizen Suits against States After *Seminole Tribe*," 27 *Envtl. L. Rev.* 935 (1997).

ordinarily enough to allege unconstitutional acts: See *Idaho v. Coeur d'Alene Tribe*, 521 U.S. 261, 281 (1997).

suit for money damages against a state officer is suit against the state: *Edelman v. Jordan*, 415 U.S. 651 (1974).

the wrong way 'round: See Pamela S. Karlan, "The Irony of Immunity: The Eleventh Amendment, Irreparable Injury and Section 1983," 53 *Stan. L. Rev.* 1311, 1328–29 (2001).

suit against state officer for violating state law is suit against the state: *Pennhurst State School and Hospital v. Haldeman*, 465 U.S. 89 (1984).

The fourteenth amendment does not apply to individuals.: *Civil Rights Cases*, 109 U.S. 3 (1883).

"a well-recognized irony": *Florida Dep't of State v. Treasure Salvors, Inc.*, 458 U.S. 670, 685 (1982); **"the rule … is one of the cornerstones":** id.

"obvious fiction": *Idaho v. Coeur d'Alene Tribe*, 521 U.S. 261 at 270; **"a careful balancing":** id. at 278 (Kennedy, J., joined by Rehnquist, C. J.); **"case-by-case approach":** id. at 280 (Kennedy, J., joined by

Rehnquist, C. J.); **the individual state defendants:** See *Coeur d'Alene Tribe v. State of Idaho,* 42 F.3d 1244 (9th Cir. 1994).

a formal exception...When Congress appropriately exercises its power under section 5: *Fitzpatrick v. Bitzer,* 427 U.S. 445 (1976).

the Supreme Court's power to review decisions of state courts: *Martin v. Hunter's Lessee,* 14 U.S. (1 Wheat.) 304 (1816).

the Supreme Court's power over federal questions where the state is a litigant: e.g., *Secretary of State of Maryland v. Munson Co., Inc.,* 467 U.S. 947 (1984).

removal to federal court of cases where the state is a litigant: e.g., *Georgia v. Rachel,* 384 U.S. 780 (1966).

power of the United States to sue a state: *United States v. Mississippi,* 380 U.S. 128, 140 (1965).

Towns, etc., are not states: *Alden v. Maine,* 527 U.S. 706 at 756; *Lincoln County v. Luning,* 133 U.S. 529 (1890).

The University of California has the immunity of the state: *Regents of the University of California v. Doe,* 519 U.S. 425 (1997); "an arm of the state": id. at 427.

A tug on the Erie Canal: Suit against the steam tug *Charlotte* for damages caused by it on the Erie Canal to boats owned by the plaintiffs was barred by "the fundamental rule" of sovereign immunity of which the eleventh amendment was "but an exemplification," because the true defendant was the state superintendent of public works, who had leased the tug; the tug itself had been returned to its owners; and the judgment could have been satisfied out of any property owned by the state. *Ex parte State of New York, No. 1,* 256 U.S. 490, 497 (1921).

the many state agencies, such as the Barbering and Cosmetology Program: *Cornwell v. California Board of Barbering and Cosmetology,* 962 F. Supp. 1260 (1997); **California School for the Blind:** See *Doe* *by Gonzalez v. Maher*, 793 F.2d 1470, 1493 (1986) (stating that earlier case, *Students for California School for the Blind v. Honig*, 736 F.2d 538 (9th Cir. 1984) *rev'd on other grounds* 471 U.S. 148 (1985), permitting suit for money damages, is no longer controlling); **California School for the Deaf:** See *Sutton v. Utah State School for the Deaf and Blind*, 173 F.3d 1226 (10th Cir. 1999); **Horse Racing Board:** See *Stamps v. Whitehouse*, 168 F.3d 501 (9th Cir. 1999) (unpublished panel opinion available on WESTLAW at 1999 WL 50867) (finding suit against members of Racing Board to be barred by either eleventh amendment or qualified immunity); cf, *Cabazon Band of Mission Indians v. Wilson*, 124 F.3d 1050 (9th Cir. 1997) (finding eleventh amendment immunity was waived by compacts entered into with Indian tribes); **the lottery:** *Scott v. California State Lotto*, 19 F.3d 1441 (9th Cir. 1994) (unpublished panel opinion available on WESTLAW at 1994 WL 87676).

"in common usage": *Will v. Michigan Dep't of State Police*, 491 U.S. 58, 64 (1989).

Cities are not states for immunity purposes but are for fourteenth amendment enforcement: *Monell v. Dep't of Social Services*, 436 U.S. 658 (1978).

"our longstanding interpretive presumption": *Vermont Agency of Natural Resources v. United States ex. rel. Stevens*, 529 U.S. 765, 780 (2000); **"a personal privilege which it may waive ...":** *College Savings Bank v. Florida Prepaid Postsecondary Education Board*, 527 U.S. 666, 675 (1999) (quoting *Clark v. Barnard*, 108 U.S. 436, 447 (1883)).

"central to sovereign dignity": *Alden v. Maine*, 527 U.S. 706 at 715.

"it is necessary to distinguish a prince from his subjects": William Blackstone, *Commentaries on the Laws of England. A Facsimile of the First Edition of 1765–1769* (Chicago: University of Chicago Press, 1979), 1, 234. For a full-bodied exposition of a prince's superiority, penned by a prince himself, see James I, Address to Parliament (1610), James I, *The Political Works of James I* (New York: Russell & Russell, 1965; reprint of the edition of 1616), 307–308:

"Kings are justly called Gods, for that they exercise a man-
ner or resemblance of Divine power upon earth; for if you
will consider the Attributes of God, you shall see how they
agree in the person of a King. God hath power to create, or
destroy, make or unmake, at his pleasure, to give life, or send
to death, to judge all, and to be judged nor accountable to
none: To raise low things, and to make high things low at his
pleasure, and to God are both soule and body due. And the
like power have Kings."

This exaggerated language was immediately corrected by what
followed: it applied only before the time that kingdoms with laws
were established.

Now "every just King in a settled Kingdom is bound to observe
that paction made to his people by his Lawes....And therefore a
King governing in a settled Kingdome, leaves to be a King, and de-
generates into a Tyrant, as soone as he leaves off to rule according to
his Lawes." James I, A Speech to Both the Houses of Parliament,
March 21, 1609, *The Political Works of James I*, reprint of the edition
of 1616 with an introduction by Charles Howard McIlwain (Cambridge: Harvard University Press, 1918), 307–309.

Jean Bodin is credited with making the concept of sovereignty
"a central feature of Western political thought." Kenneth Douglas
McRae, "Introduction," in Jean Bodin, *The Six Books of a Common-
weale*. A facsimile reprint of the English translation of 1606, corrected
and supplemented (Cambridge: Harvard University Press, 1962), 14.
Sovereignty, in Bodin's sense, cannot be applied to the fifty states, for
just as God cannot make another god, so a sovereign cannot make
another sovereign. Book the First, chapter X. Nor is Congress a sovereign because a power "for a certain time limited" is not sovereignty,
but is in trust and accountable. Id., chapter VIII. A prince can be a
sovereign but he is bound "by the laws of God and nature" and is
also obliged to observe the oath he has made to keep the laws of his
country. Id. For this author, sovereignty does not imply immunity.
The sovereign is "the debtor of justice and so bound to give every man

his due." Id. at 106. Bodin gives examples of judgments entered by "the court of Paris" against the kings of France. Id. at 111.

"threaten the financial integrity": *Alden*, 527 U.S. 706 at 750. For a detailed critique of the paragraph setting out this reason, see David McGowan, "Judicial Writing and the Ethics of the Judicial Office," *Georgetown Journal of Legal Ethics*, 14, 558–565 (2001).

Acknowledging that the Supreme Court has not presented "any functional justifications for its decisions in this area" and that they seem to signify "nothing except a weirdly anthropomorphic desire to protect states' 'dignity,'" Roderick M. Hills Jr., offers a new, subtle, and tentative rationale. See Hills, "The Eleventh Amendment as Curb on Bureaucratic Power," 53 Stan. L. Rev. 1225,1226, 1229 (2001). It is that if states were liable for damages, the costs would be borne by the general finances of the state rather than by the particular state agencies that caused them, and that particular agencies might negligently pay excessive claims because their own budgets would not feel the cost. Id. at 1234. As Hills admits, the argument does not have empirical proof.

"the omnipresent teacher": *Olmstead v. United States*, 277 U.S. 438, 485 (1928). (Brandeis, J., dissenting).

federal law will be shaped by members of congress: See Larry D. Kramer, "Putting Politics Back into the Political Safeguards of Federalism," 100 *Colum. L. Rev.* 215 (2000).

"Behind the words: *Monaco*, 292 U.S. 313 at 322; *immunity inherent: id.* 1329; **a "presupposition":** *Blatchford*, 501 U.S. 775 at 779; **"the background principle:** *Seminole Tribe*, 517 U.S. 44 at 72.

modern justices attached to the text: e.g., *Minnesota v. Carter*, 525 U.S. 83, 91–92 (1998) (Scalia and Thomas, JJ., concurring); *Attorney General of New York v. Soto-Lopez*, 476 U.S. 898 (920) (O'Connor, J.). See also Antonin Scalia, *A Matter of Interpretation: Federal Courts and the Law* (Princeton: Princeton University Press, 1997), 23–25.

CHAPTER 3

VOTARIES

the Supreme Court distinguishes cities: e.g., *Monell v. Dep't of Social Services of New York City*, 436 U.S. 658 (1978).

State law bound the state to pay: *Reis v. State*, 133 Cal. 593, 65 P. 1102 (1901); cf. *Union Trust Co. of San Francisco v. State of California*, 154 Cal. 716, 727, 99 P. 183 (1908).

"In the winter and spring of 1976, the State of New York": Felix Rohatyn, "Fiscal Disaster The City Can't Face Alone," *New York Times*, October 9, 2001, Sec. A, p. 35.

employment discrimination and tort cases: *Regents of the University of California v. Doe*, 519 U.S. 425 (1997) (employment contract dispute); *Lujan v. Regents of the University of California*, 69 F.3d 1511 (10th Cir. 1995) (tort).

waive it and win . . . on the merits: See e.g., *Katz v. Regents of the University of California*, 229 F.3d 831 (9th Cir. 2000).

It works in patent cases: *Regents of the University of California v. Genentech, Inc.*, 527 U.S. 1031 (1999); **settlement of case:** Marcia Barinago, "Genentech, UC Settle Suit for $200 Million," *Science* 286 (November 26, 1999) 1655.

U.C. was immune [although] acting as manager for the . . . federal government. *Regents of the University of California v. Doe*, 519 U.S. at 431.

Georgia Medicaid case: *McClendon v. Georgia Dep't of Community Health*, 261 F.3d 1252 (11th Cir. 2001).

how John Marshall explained . . . the eleventh amendment: *Cohens v. Virginia*, 19 U.S. (6 Wheat.) 264, 406–407 (1821).

The history of *Chisholm v. Georgia*, 2 U.S. (2 Dall.) 419 (1793): *The Documentary History of the Supreme Court of the United States,*

1789–1800, vol. 5, *Suits against the States*, ed. Maeva Marcus (New York: Columbia University Press, 1994), 127–137.

"The supreme court shall have exclusive jurisdiction...": U.S. Stat. 1: 81–82.

At common law an individual could not sue the sovereign: *Chisholm*, 2 U.S. (2 Dall.) 419 at 448; **"let me hope and pray,..."**: id. at 436; **"A dispute between A and B..."**: id. at 450; **"reduce states to mere corporations..."**: id. at 468; **"To the Constitution of the United States the term SOVEREIGN is totally unknown."**: id. at 454; **"that a state, any more than the men who compose it..."**: id. at 456; **"to establish justice"**: id. at 465; **Could a citizen not sue in the same way?**: id. at 472; **the United States ...was bound by the law of nations:** id. at 473–474.

Georgia settled: See *The Documentary History*, 136.

Congress at once proposed the eleventh amendment...: id. at 137. **the eleventh...tells the judges how to construe part of article III:** For a seminal review of the eleventh amendment and its proper construction, see William A. Fletcher, "A Historical Interpretation of the Eleventh Amendment: A Narrow Construction of an Affirmative Grant of Jurisdiction Rather than a Prohibition against Jurisdiction," 35 *Stan. L. Rev.* 1033 (1983).

Marbury v. Madison: 1 Cranch 137 (1803).

"the passive-aggressive approach": Mark A. Graber, "The Passive Aggressive Virtues: *Cohens v. Virginia* and the Problematic Establishment of Judicial Power," *Constitutional Commentary* 12 (1995) 67; **"not fond of butting against a wall"**: Marshall to Joseph Story, September 26, 1823, quoted in id., 86; **the first names of the defendants:** id. at 75; **the prosecution of the brothers and $100 fine:** *Cohens v. Virginia*, 19 U.S. (6 Wheat.) 264 (1821); **motion to dismiss denied:** id.

"over all Cases...": U.S. constitution, art. III; **"This clause extends the jurisdiction...to all the cases:** *Cohens*, 19 U.S. (6 Wheat.) 264

at 378; **states had given their consent:** id. at 382; **"spirit of the constitution":** id. at 383; **"whoever may be the parties":** id. at 392; **eleventh amendment did not apply to an appeal:** id., 407–411; **nor to suit by state's own citizens:** id., 412.

"remarkable state paper": Albert J. Beveridge, *The Life of John Marshall* (Boston: Houghton Mifflin Company, 1919), iv, 342.

judgment of borough court affirmed: *Cohens*, 19 U.S. (6 Wheat.) 264 at 447.

McCullough v. Maryland, 17 U.S. (4 Wheat.) 316 (1819); **Ohio statute of February 1819:** *Osborn v. Bank of the United States*, 22 U.S. (9 Wheat.) 738, 740 (1824); **the $100,000 collected:** Richard H. Fallon, Daniel J. Meltzer, and David L. Shapiro, *Hart and Wechsler's The Federal Courts and the Federal System* (Westbury, N.Y.: The Foundation Press, 1996), 1049; **"The party named in the record":** *Osborn*, 22 U.S. (9 Wheat.) 733 at 857.

"It is a mistake, that the constitution was not designed to operate upon states": *Martin v. Hunter's Lessee*, 14 U.S. (1 Wheat.) 304 at 343. **"It is crowded with provisions that restrain or annul the sovereignty ... ":** id.

ordered the prisoner freed: *Worcester v. Georgia*, 31 U.S. 6 (1832). Where a suit was on the record against the governor of a state in his official capacity and the object of the suit was the recovery of money and property, Chief Justice Marshall explicitly noted that no federal law was invoked and dismissed the suit. *Governor of Georgia v. Madrazo*, 26 U.S. (6 Pet.) 110 (1828).

"the administration of the fiscal affairs of the state": *Louisiana ex rel. Elliott v. Jumel*, 107 U.S. 711, 722 (1883).

the suit by New Hampshire and New York: *New Hampshire v. Louisiana*, 108 U.S. 76 (1883).

"a valid obligation of the state": Constitution of the state of Louisiana, as amended by the act of January 24, 1874, and quoted in *Hans v. Louisiana*, 134 U.S. 1 at 2 (1890).

"anomalous and unheard of": id. at 18; "the letter": id. at 15.

"It is inherent in the nature of sovereignty...": Alexander Hamilton, Number 81, *The Federalist.*

"It is not in the power of individuals...": James Madison, Speech, *Debates in the Several State Convention*, ed. Jonathan Elliot (1888; reprint, New York: Burt Franklin), 3, 533.

"It is not rational to suppose...": John Marshall, Speech, id. at 555.

"extrajudicial": *Hans*, 134 U.S. 1 at 20; *Chisholm* wrongly decided: id. at 13–14.

Hans read to enlarge the eleventh: See e.g., *Board of Trustees of the University of Alabama v. Garrett*, 531 U.S. 356, 363, (2001); speculation as to natural law basis: *Alden*, 527 U.S. at 773, 795 n.30 (Souter, J., dissenting).

"writers on public law": *Hans*, 134 U.S. 1 at 21; their reliance on custom or common law: id. at 16 (referring to Justice Iredell's opinion in *Chisholm v. Georgia*, 2 U.S. 419, 437–446 (1793) in which Justice Iredell sets out the English common law heritage. Justice Bradley cites no "writers on public law" and his authorities consist of a letter by Daniel Webster and citations to other Supreme Court opinions.

"State" as a term given sense in a system: See H. L. A. Hart, "Definition and Theory in Jurisprudence," in his *Essays in Jurisprudence and Philosophy* (Oxford: The Clarendon Press, 1983), 41–43.

thirty-six states were never sovereign: See George Fletcher, *Our Secret Constitution. How Lincoln Redefined American Democracy* (New York: Oxford University Press, 2001), 117; "equal footing": e.g., *United States v. Louisiana*, 339 U.S. 699, 703 (1950); *Stearns v. Minnesota*, 179 U.S. 223, 243 (1990).

the state in Hobbes: See Thomas Hobbes, *Leviathan*, ed. Richard Tuck (Cambridge: Cambridge University Press, 1991), chapter 18, pp. 125–128; **God in Calvin:** The translation into English of John Calvin's *Institutio Christianae religionis* by John Allen in 1813 and again by Henry Beveridge, himself a lawyer, in 1845 used the terms "sovereign" and "sovereignty" to convey Calvin's meaning more clearly. See Calvin, *Institutes of the Christian Religion*, trans. Ford Lewis Battles (Philadelphia: The Westminster Press, 1960), 121, n.1. Sovereignty is a way of putting God's omnipotence, emphasized, for example, in ibid., book I, xvi, 3. See also Gisbert Beyerhaus, *Studien zur staatsanschauung Calvins, mit besonderer berücksichtigung seines souveränitätsbegriffs* (Berlin: Trowitzsch & Sohn, 1910), 58.

on the religion of Joseph Bradley: See Joseph Bradley, "Esoteric Thoughts on Religion and Religionism," in *Miscellaneous Writings*, ed. Charles Bradley (Newark, N.J.: L. J. Hardhan, 1902), 431.

on Holmes: See John T. Noonan Jr., *Persons and Masks of the Law* (New York: Farrar, Straus and Giroux, 1978) (discussing *American Banana Co. v. United Fruit Co.*, 213 U.S. 347 (1909)); **"the authority that makes the law ...":** *The Western Maid*, 257 U.S. 419, 432 (1922); **"the logical and practical ground that there can be no legal right ...":** *Kawananakoa v. Polyblank*, 205 U.S. 349, 353 (1907).

Hans **as break with precedent:** See John V. Orth, *The Judicial Power of the United States* (New York: Oxford University Press, 1987), 62–63, 79.

reconciliation with the South as motive for *Hans:* id. at 79; cf. Eric Foner, *Reconstruction* (New York: Harper and Row, 1988), 580–581; Pamela Brandwein, *Reconstructing Reconstruction: The Supreme Court and the Production of Historical Truth* (Durham, N.C.: Duke University Press, 1999), 8–17.

the historical explanation objected to: See *Seminole Tribe of Florida v. Florida*, 517 U.S. 44, 68–69 (1996) ("undocumented and highly speculative extralegal explanation").

"the trial of controversies in which the States may be parties": James Madison, Number 39, *The Federalist*; **controversies relating to "the boundaries"**: id.; **"residuary and inviolable"**: id. Madison's statements here, published January 16, 1788, and his similar remarks at the Virginia convention that opened June 2, 1788, are interpreted by James E. Pfander to refer to the original jurisdiction language of article III; see Pfander, "Rethinking the Supreme Court's Original Jurisdiction in State-Party Cases," 82 *Calif. L. Rev.* 555, 633, n.318.

"[u]ltimate authority resides in the people alone": James Madison, Number 46, *The Federalist*; **federalizing state courts**: id.

"perhaps not less essential": Alexander Hamilton, Number 80, *The Federalist*, "The Powers of the Judiciary"; **"[u]nless, therefore, there is a surrender"**: id., Number 81; **"the proper objects" of the federal courts**: Hamilton, Number 80; *The Federalist*.

"The truth is that difficulties on this point are inherent...": "Alexander Hamilton, "Opinion as to the Constitutionality of the Bank of the United States," February 23, 1791, in *The Works of Alexander Hamilton*, ed. Henry Cabot Lodge (New York: G. P. Putnam's Sons, 1904), 3, 457; **"the literal meaning"**: id.; **"the end..."**: id., 458 (italics in original).

a **"corrupt squadron"**: Thomas Jefferson to George Washington, May 23, 1792, in *The Papers of Thomas Jefferson*, ed. Charles T. Cullen (1990) 23, 537; **"How shall it be determined which side is right? There are some things..."**: Hamilton to Washington, August 18, 1792, in *The Papers of Alexander Hamilton*, ed. Harold C. Syrett (New York: Columbia University Press, 1967), 12, 251; **"the Antifederal Champions"**: id., 258; **"That the beneficial effects ..."**: id. I am indebted to Professor David McGowan for focusing on "the middle ground" as "the middle ground of sovereignty." See David McGowan, "Ethos in Law and History: Alexander Hamilton, *The Federalist*, and the Supreme Court," 85 *Minn. L. Rev.* 755, 804 (2001).

"credulous votaries...": Hamilton, Number 60, *The Federalist.*

"We, the people of the Confederate States...": Constitution of the Confederate States of America, Preamble.

"between a State and citizens of another State": id.

the vigor and vitality of true development: John Henry Newman, *An Essay on the Development of Christian Doctrine*, ed. Charles Frederick Harold (London: Longmans, Green and Co., 1949), 158 (corruption), 165–171 (continuity), 189–191 (vigor).

CHAPTER 4

THE SOVEREIGN PUBLISHER AND THE LAST OF THE MENU GIRLS

Peter Roberts's patent: U.S. Patent No. 4,722,055, "Methods and Apparatus for Funding Future Liability of Uncertain Cost" (issued January 26, 1988).

"the most excruciating case-by-case basis": Robert L. Harmon, *Patents and the Federal Circuit*, (Washington D.C., Bureau of National Affairs, 3d ed., (1994)), 39.

useful and new: 35 U.S.C. §101; **a "new use":** 35 U.S.C. §100b.

the University of Michigan plan: George J. Schwatzer to the U.S. Dep't of Education's Student Financial Assistance Program, February 3, 1999, http://arizona.collegesavings.com/azbreq.shtml.

The Florida legislation: Fla. Stat. ch. 240.551; **the marketing entity:** id., sec. 5(b); **product providers:** id., sec. 6(f); **no liability for misrepresentation:** id., sec. 6(d); **extension to qualified private universities:** id., sec. 10; **advertising slogan:** Florida Prepaid College Program website http://www.fsba.state.fl.us/prepaid/Main-Frame.htm; **success of program and comparison with CSB:** Tommy Sangchompuphen, "College Prepayment Plan Is Focus of Patent Suit against Florida," *Wall Street Journal*, July 10, 1995, sec. B, p. 3.

On occasion a state or a state agency...was sued: *Jacobs Wind Elec. Co., Inc. v. Florida Dep't of Transp.*, 919 F.2d 726 (Fed. Cir. 1990) (holding that eleventh amendment barred suit by Florida resident alleging that Florida Department of Transportation infringed on plaintiff's patent on tidal flow system because Congress failed to enunciate clearly in the text of the patent laws that it intended to abrogate the states' sovereign immunity); *Chew v. State of Cal.*, 893 F.2d 331 (Fed. Cir. 1990) (holding for the same reason that eleventh amendment barred plaintiff's patent infringement suit against the state of California alleging infringement of her patent for a method for testing automobile exhaust emissions); *Watts v. University of Del.*, 622 F.2d 47 (3d Cir. 1980) (holding that a fact issue existed as to whether use of chair frame in dormitory lounge was for experimental purposes, precluding summary judgment for university as an arm of the state on the theory that frame was in public use more than one year before filing of patent application for chair design); *Lemelson v. Ampex Corp.*, 372 F. Supp. 708 (N.D. Ill. 1974) (denying a motion to dismiss a claim against a state for contributory infringement because the state had waived its immunity); *Hercules, Inc. v. Minnesota State Highway Dep't*, 337 F. Supp. 795 (D. Minn. 1972) (holding that state highway department was subject to suit for injunctive relief but was not subject to liability damages, in absence of waiver by state of its eleventh amendment immunity in suit by plaintiff for alleged infringement of a patent for process of applying weed-and pest-control spray); *William C. Popper & Co. v. Pennsylvania Liquor Control Bd.*, 16 F. Supp. 762 (E.D. Pa. 1936) (dismissing a claim against the state for patent infringement as barred by the eleventh amendment's grant of state immunity); *Automobile Abstract & Title Co. v. Haggerty*, 46 F.2d 86 (E.D. Mich. 1931) (dismissing claim against highway commission for infringement of plaintiff's patent for pavement due to the state's sovereign immunity under the eleventh amendment); *Warren Bros. Co. v. Kibbe*, 43 F.2d 582 (D. Ore. 1925) (holding that state had waived its immunity against patent infringement suit after agreeing to indemnify contractors for royalties owed when infringing patents for paving materials).

Supreme Court emphasis on need for explicit override: *Atascadero State Hosp. v. Scanton*, 473 U.S. 234, 243 (1985); **the doubt became a certainty:** *Jacobs Wind Elec. Co. v. Florida Dep't of Transp.*, 919 F.2d 726, 728 (Fed. Cir. 1990).

"whoever includes...": 35 U.S.C. §271(h); **"Any State...shall not be immune..."**: id. §296(a).

reasoning of affirmance: *College Savings Bank v. Florida Prepaid Postsecondary Education Expense Board*, 148 F.3d 1343 (Fed. Cir. 1998) (Clevenger, J., with Rader and Bryson, JJ., concurring). See also *College Savings Bank v. Florida Prepaid Postsecondary Education Expense Board*, 131 F.3d 353 (3d Cir. 1997) (Greenberg, J., with Mansmann and Alarcon, JJ., concurring).

"a history of 'widespread and persisting deprivation...'": *Florida Prepaid Postsecondary Education Expense Board v. College Savings Bank*, 527 U.S. 627, 645 (1999), per Rehnquist, C.J., joined by O'Connor, Scalia, Kennedy, and Thomas, JJ., quoting *Boerne*, 521 U.S. 507 at 626; **statute disproportionate:** id. at 641–647; **the statute defended:** id. at 654–664 (Stevens, J., dissenting, joined by Souter, Ginsburg, and Breyer, JJ.).

existing patent law largely preempted the state courts: The patent laws preempt inconsistent state laws. See *Compco Corp. v. Day Brite Lighting Inc.*, 376 U.S. 234 (1964). State contract and unfair competition laws can offer some degree of protection beyond the patent laws without being preempted. See *Bonito Boats, Inc. v. Thunder Craft Boats, Inc.*, 489 U.S. 141, 165 (1989) ("Both the law of unfair competition and state trade secret law have coexisted harmoniously with federal patent protection for almost 200 years, and Congress has given no indication that their operation is inconsistent with the operation of the federal patent laws."); *Lear Inc. v. Adkins*, 395 U.S. 653, 674–676 (1969) (permitting state court to provide limited contract law protection in dispute surrounding patent). Contract and trade secrets laws depend on some relationship between the parties. While patent laws protect the inventor against the world, state unfair competition laws merely prevent improper acquisition, use, or disclosure of secrets used in a business. See Restatement of Unfair Competition Law §39 cmt. c (distinguishing federal patent from state protection). Because the patent at issue in *Florida Prepaid* had already been granted and there was no relationship between the parties, it is unlikely that CSB could be afforded state law protection. See id. (publication by patent office deprives trade practice of secrecy necessary for protection).

What proportion could be more exact?: It could be argued that the Supreme Court supposed that there would be groundless patent suits ("strike suits" in legal jargon), so there would be more suits than actual infringements. But the remedy for strike suits is judicial vigilance, not invalidation of an act of Congress.

"Truly bizarre": Charles Fried, "Supreme Court Folly," *New York Times*, July 6, 1999, sec. A, p. 17; **"Bizarre":** James N. Gardner, **"The Supreme Court's War on Intellectual Property,"** *Nature Biotechnology*, January 18, 2000, 1001; **"potentially devastating":** id.; **"bizarre":** David Malakoff, "Critics Say Rulings Give State U. License to Steal, *Science*, September 29, 2000, 2267.

"adequate remuneration" for governmental use of a patent: World Trade Organization, Agreement on Trade-Related Aspects of Intellectual Property Rights, April 15, 1994.

"Evenhandedness" could not be expected.: *College Savings Bank v. Florida Prepaid Postsecondary Education Expense Board*, 527 U.S. 669, 688 (1999) (Scalia, J., joined by Rehnquist, C.J., and O'Connor, Kennedy, and Thomas, JJ.); **"might well have dropped from the lips of Robespierre":** id. at 696; **"in ordinary commercial ventures":** id. at 694 (dissent, Breyer, J., joined by Stevens, Souter, and Ginsburg, JJ.); **foreign sovereign immunity as test:** id. at 692 (per Stevens, J.), cf. the Foreign Sovereign Immunities Act, 28 U.S.C. §1605. The earlier history of the case: 131 F.3d 353 (3d Cir. 1998) (Greenberg, J., joined by Mansmann and Alarcon, JJ.), affirming

948 F. Supp. 400 (D.N.J. 1996) (Brown, J.); The Trademark Remedy Clarification Act: 106 Stat. 3567 (1992).

No case where a state has been successfully sued for infringement of a trademark; see, e.g. *State Contracting & Engineering Corp. v. State of Florida*, 258 F .3d 1329 (Fed. Cir. 2001) (suit for patent and trademark infringement and for taking of property dismissed on sovereign immunity grounds*); Idaho Potato Commission v. M & M Produce Farm & Sales*, 95 F. Supp. 2d 150 (S.D.N.Y. 2000) (Idaho Potato Commission held to enjoy sovereign immunity in suit involving trademark claims).

Chávez's suit: *Chávez v. Arte Publico*, 59 F.3d 539 (5th Cir. 1995), applying the Copyright Remedy Clarification Act, 17 U.S.C. §511(a); reversed, 157 F.3d 282 (5th Cir. 1998) (on remand from the Supreme Court, reversing the district court); **"Are you so sure?":** id. at 298 n.54 (Wisdom, J., dissenting); **en banc ordered:** 178 F.3d 281; **"the kind of massive constitutional violations":** 204 F.3d 601, 607 (5th Cir. 2000); **the origin of Arte Publico:** http://www.arte.uh.edu/Arte_Publico_Press/arte_publico_press .html. Chávez had sued for a declaratory judgment and an injunction as well as for money damages. After her claim for damages was dismissed, Arte Publico settled her suit for an injunction. Communication from Kenneth Kuffner, counsel for Chávez, October 29, 2001. Citing *College Savings Bank*, a district court dismissed a suit against the John D. Calandra Italian American Institute and City University of New York, held to be "arms of the State." *Salerno v. City University*, 2001 WL 1267158 (S.D.N.Y. 2001).

CHAPTER 5

PERHAPS INCONSEQUENTIAL PROBLEMS

"arbitrary discrimination": Secretary of Labor, *The Older American Worker. Age Discrimination in Employment* (1965), reproduced in U.S.

Equal Opportunity Employment Commission, *Legislative History of the Age Discrimination in Employment Act* (Washington: U.S. Government Printing Office, 1981), 10 (hereafter *History*); **no hostility but preference for young:** Ibid., 23; **reasons for preference:** ibid., 28–29, 33; **age limits:** ibid., 23; effect of discrimination: ibid., 35–36; **recommendation:** 37.

the presidential message, January 23, 1967: Report of the Committee on Education and Labor, H.R. 805, 90th Cong., 1st Sess, in *History*, 75.

the ADEA: Pub. L. 90–202, 81 Stat. 602 (December 15, 1967) codified as amended at 29 U.S.C. §631–634.

ageism "as great an evil…": Special Message of the President to Congress on Older Americans, 1972 Pub. Papers 461, 483 (March 23, 1972).

140 suits, six thousand investigations: Special Committee on the Ageing, United States Senate, "Improving the Age Discrimina-tion Law" (September 1973), in *History*, 222–223; "a good idea": id. at 223.

not "a conscious decision": House Report No. 93–690, "Fair Labor Standards Amendments of 1974," 93rd Cong., 2d Sess., in *History*, 251.

Congress in 1978 barred mandatory retirement: Age Discrimination in Employment Act Amendments of 1978, Pub. L. 95–256, 92 Stat. 189; **In 1986,** ADEA again amended: Age Discrimination in Employment Act Amendments of 1986, Pub. L. 99–592, 100 Stat. 3342; **exemption for tenured professors:** id. at §6.

Allegations of MacPherson and Narz: *Kimel v. Florida Board of Regents*, 528 U.S. 62, 69 (2000); **of Kimel and his co-plaintiffs:** ibid., 70; **of Dickson:** ibid., 70–71; **Eleventh Circuit decision:** *Kimel v. State of Florida Board of Regents*, 139 F.3d 1426 (11th Cir. 1998); **"not a proportional response":** id. at 1447; **"simply thought it was a good idea":** ibid. at 1448.

Circuit split: Compare *Cooper v. New York State Office of Mental Health*, 162 F.3d 770 (2d Cir. 1998) (holding ADEA valid exercise of congressional power); *Migneault v. Peck*, 158 F.3d 1131 (10th Cir. 1998) (same); *Coger v. Board of Regents of the State of Tennessee*, 154 F.3d 296 (6th Cir. 1998) (same); *Keeton v. University of Nevada System*, 150 F.3d 1055 (9th Cir. 1998) (same); *Scott v. University of Mississippi*, 148 F.3d 493 (5th Cir. 1998) (same); *Goshtasby v. Board of Trustees of the University of Illinois*, 141 F.3d 761 (7th Cir. 1998) (same), with *Humenanusk v. Regents of the University of Minnesota*, 152 F.3d 822 (8th Cir. 1998); *Kimmel*, 139 F.3d 1426 (11th Cir. 1998). Seven of the eight circuit cases were suits against state universities.

abrogation of immunity: *Kimel*, 528 U.S. 62 at 74; **Congress failed the** *Boerne* **tests:** id. at 82–91 (opinion by O'Connor, J., joined by Rehnquist, C.J., and Scalia, Kennedy, and Thomas, JJ., Kennedy and Thomas, however, finding no abrogation).

state police retired at age fifty-eight: *Massachusetts Board of Retirement v. Murgia*, 427 U.S. 307 (1976); **It was ... an unfortunate fact of life ...:** *Gregory v. Ashcroft*, 501 U.S. 452, 472 (1991); **"It is far from true":** id. at 473.

"substantially higher burdens on state employers": *Kimel*, 528 U.S. 62 at 87; **Congress had not "identified any ... discrimination that rose ...:** id. at 89; **"Congress had virtually no reason ...":** id. at 91; **"an unwarranted response":** id. at 89; **court explicitly reproving dissenters:** id. at 79–80. For criticism, see A. Christopher Bryant and Timothy J. Simeone, "Remanding to Congress: The Supreme Court's New 'On the Record' Constitutional Reviews of Federal Statutes," 86 *Cornell L. Rev.* 328, 375–383 (2001). The court suggested that its decision was not "the end of the line" for the plaintiffs, there might be other remedies they could pursue. *Kimel*, 528 U.S. 62 at 91. A subsequent inquiry found no other remedies available to the Alabama plaintiffs. See Evelyn Corrine McCafferty, "Age Discrimination and Sovereign Immunity: Does *Kimel*

Signal the End of the Line for Alabama's State Employees?" 52 *Ala. L. Rev.* 1057 (2001).

"profoundly misguided": *Kimel*, 528 U.S. 62 at 97 (dissent by Stevens, J., joined by Souter, Ginsburg, and Breyer, JJ.).

as Brandeis had pointed out: *Burnet v. Coronado Oil & Gas Co.*, 285 U.S. 393, 406–410 (1932).

"policy choice": *Kimel*, 528 U.S. 62 at 96 (dissent).

"reasonably prophylactic": id. at 88 (opinion of court); **"entitled to much deference":** id. at 81; **"that merely parrots:** id. at 86; **"a somewhat broader swath":** id. at 81.

Thomas Jefferson believed in the inferiority: See Thomas Jefferson, *Notes on the State of Virginia* (Williamsburg: Institute of Early American History and Culture, 1955), 138–143.

Why should what was "probably not true" be taken as the basis for discrimination treated as rational?: See similar criticism in Note, "The Irrational Application of Rational Basis. *Kimel, Garrett* and Congressional Power to Abrogate State Sovereign Immunity," 114 *Harv. L. Rev.* 2146, n.55, citing Larry Alexander, "What Makes Wrongful Discrimination Wrong? Preference, Stereotypes and Process," 141 *U. Pa. L. Rev.* 149, 169–170 (1992), and Cass R. Sunstein, "Three Civil Rights Fallacies," 79 *Calif. L. Rev.* 751, 752 (1991).

"discrete and insular minority": *United States v. Carolene Products Co.*, 304 U.S. 144, 152, n.4 (1938).

"all persons, if they live out their normal life spans": *Kimel*, 528 U.S. 62 at 83.

Americans with Disabilities Act: 42 U.S.C. §§12101–12213; **congressional findings:** 42 U.S.C. §12101(a).

As early as 1920: An Act to provide for the Promotion of Vocational Rehabilitation of Persons Disabled in Industry or Otherwise and Their Return to Civil Employment, 41 Stat. 735 (June 2, 1920); **by 1988 ten federal acts were in place:** Fair Housing Amendments of 1988,

42 U.S.C. §3604; Protection and Advocacy for Mentally Ill Individuals Act of 1986, 42 U.S.C. §10801; Air Carrier Access Act of 1986, 49 U.S.C. §41705; Voting Accessibility for the Elderly and Handicapped Act, 42 U.S.C. §1973ee et seq.; Developmental Disabilities Assistance and Bill of Rights, 42 U.S.C. §6000 et seq.; Education of the Handicapped Act, Pub. L. 91–561m, Title VI, 84 Stat. 175 (reenacted in 1990 as the Individuals with Disabilities Education Act, 20 U.S.C. §1400 et seq.); Rehabilitation Act of 1973, 29 U.S.C. §701 et seq.; Architectural Barriers Act of 1968, 42 U.S.C. §4151 et seq.; also the Urban Mass Transportation Act of 1970, 49 U.S.C. §4151 et seq. and the National Housing Act Amendments Act of 1975, 12 U.S.C. §1701 et seq., both mentioned in House of Representatives, Report 101–485 (1990), pt. 3:25 n.10 (hereafter House Report 101–485).

Task force on the Rights and Empowerment of Americans with Disabilities: see House Report 101–485, pt. 2:27(task force established by the subcommittee on Select Education); **"massive, society-wide":** See e.g., Senate Report 101–116 at 9 (1990).

nineteen hearings: See House Report 101–485 pt. 2: 24–25 (listing twelve days of hearings by the Committee on Education and Labor and its subcommittees and those testifying); House Report 101–485 pt. 4: 28–29 (listing two days of hearings by Committee on Energy and Commerce and those testifying); Senate Report 101–116 at 4–5 (listing five days of hearings and those testifying). **national opinion polls:** Senate Report 101–116 at 6 (1989) (citing Louis Harris and Associates, "The ICD Survey of Disabled Americans: Bringing Disabled Americans Into the Mainstream" (1986), and Louis Harris and Associates, "The ICD Survey II: Empowering Disabled Americans" (1987)).

allegations of Patricia Garrett and Milton Ash: See Petitioner's Brief, *Bd. of Trustees v. Garrett*, available on Westlaw, 2000 WL 821035, *15–*16, Brief for Respondents Patricia Garrett and Milton Ash, *Bd. of Trustees v. Garrett*, available on Westlaw, 2000 WL

1593420, *1–*5. See also, *Morning Edition:* "Supreme Court to hear case of two disabled workers in Alabama" (NPR broadcast, October 11, 2000), available at 2000 WL 21481865.

suits dismissed: *Garrett v. Board of Trustees of the University of Alabama/Ash v. Alabama Department of Youth Services,* 989 F. Supp. 1409 (1998) (Acker, J.); **the circuit:** *Garrett v. University of Alabama at Birmingham Board of Trustees,* 193 F.3d 1214 (1999) (Roney, J., with Anderson, C. J., concurring and Cook, J., concurring in part and dissenting in part).

solicitor general: Brief for the United States, available on Westlaw, 2000 WL 1178761 (2000) ; **amici:** See e.g., Brief for the National Association of Protection and Advocacy Systems and United Cerebral Palsy Associations, Inc, available on Westlaw, 2000 WL 1154037 (2000); Brief of Amici Curiae Self-Advocates Becoming Empowered, available on Westlaw, 2000 WL 1154043 (2000).

"Although by its terms the Amendment…": *Bd. of Trustees of the University of Alabama v. Garrett,* 121 S. Ct. 955, 961–962 (2001) (Rehnquist, C. J., joined by O'Connor, Kennedy, Scalia, and Thomas, JJ.); **"these now familiar principles":** id. at 963.

"simply fails to show…": id. at 965; **"half a dozen examples":** id.; **"no pattern of unconstitutional state discrimination":** id. at 966.

"to squeeze out…": id.; **"undue hardship":** id. at 959.

the embattled four dissenters: 121 S. Ct. 955, 969 (Breyer, J., dissenting, joined by Stevens, Souter, and Ginsburg, JJ.); **"roughly 300":** id. at 970; **appendix to the dissent:** id. at 977 (Appendix C); **"a legislature is not a court of law":** id. at 970.

"Unlike courts…": id. at 973; **"on its head":** id.

"congruent": id. at 974; **"reminiscent":** id.; **the court "improperly invades…":** id. at 975–976. Another statute, whose enforceability for damages against a state became doubtful, was the Family and Medical Leave Act of 1993, 29 U.S.C. §§2601–2654. The Ninth

Circuit held that the statute was a valid exercise of section 5 power, abrogating state immunity. *Hibbs v. Department of Human Resources*, 273 F .3d 844 (9th Cir. 2001). Seven other circuits held to the contrary. See id. at 850. The Ninth Circuit reasoned that the statute was a proportionate response to the nation's long history of gender stereotyping that treated men as the providers and women as the caregivers. Id. at 861–864. The court put the burden on the state to show that the record before Congress did not support the remedy provided by the statute, stating: "Because state-sponsored gender-discrimination is presumptively unconstitutional, section 5 legislation that is intended to remedy or prevent gender discrimination is presumptively constitutional." Id. at 857.

CHAPTER 6

GANG RAPE AT STATE U.

"all persons within the United States shall have the right to be free from crimes of violence motivated by gender": Violence Against Women Act, 42 U.S.C. §13981(b).

the facts as set out by Brzonkala: Pleadings: *Brzonkala v. Virginia Polytechnic and State University*, 935 F. Supp. 772 (W.D. Va. 1996); *Brzonkala v. Virginia Polytechnic and State University*, 935 F. Supp. 779 (W.D. Va. 1996); *Brzonkala v. Virginia Polytechnic Institute and State University*, 132 F.3d 949 (4th Cir. 1997). When a court dismisses a case for failure to state a claim, it must accept the plaintiff's allegations as true before finding that they are legally insufficient. Such was the situation here. What the court accepted as true and what is stated here as fact is what the plaintiff stated in her pleadings.

Virginia Tech ranked eighth in the nation: College Football Poll, *Past Rankings: AP, UPI, USA Today*, at http://www.collegefootballpoll.com/polls_1936_2000.html.

term of imprisonment for rape in "the discretion of the court or the jury": Va. St. §18.2–61C.

Title IX of the Education Act of 1972: 20 U.S.C. §1681.

influence of the football team not indication of discrimination: 935 F. Supp. at 778; **Virginia Tech's sensitivity to victims:** id. at 777; **environment only "might become abusive in the future":** id. at 778.

a crime due to an animus based on gender: 935 F. Supp. at 789.

Lopez: *United States v. Lopez,* 514 U.S. 549 (1995).

the law unconstitutional: 935 F. Supp. at 785–789; **remedy "purely by chance":** id. at 800.

"This case arises from a gang rape...": *Brzonkala v. VPI,* 132 F.3d 949, 954 (4th Cir. 1997); **"excellent legal analysis":** id. at 974 (dissent); **"bold intransigence":** id. at 977 (dissent).

"foundational principles of our constitution": 169 F.3d 820, 826 (en banc); **"ignore vast temptations...":** id. at 897 (concurrence); **dissent:** id. at 903–933. **The en banc court remanded Brzonkala's hostile environment claim:** id. at 827, n.2.

"presumption of constitutionality": *United States v. Morrison,* 529 U.S. 598, 607 (2000) (Rehnquist, C.J., joined by O'Connor, Kennedy, Scalia, and Thomas, JJ.). The caption of the case needs explanation. Brzonkala was the named plaintiff at the district court level, and the United States intervened at the district court level to defend the constitutionality of 42 U.S.C. §13981. The U.S. then separately filed an appeal, and the Fourth Circuit consolidated the government's appeal with Brzonkala's appeal. Brzonkala and the United States then filed separate petitions for certiorari to the Supreme Court, and their cases were consolidated once again.

"coordinate branch": *Morrison,* 529 U.S. 598 at 607; **"a plain showing":** id. at 598.

the decisive swing: *NLRB v. Jones & Laughlin Steel Corp.,* 331 U.S. 416 (1937).

"latitude": *Morrison*, 529 U.S. 598 at 608; **"substantially affect"**: id. at 609.

Congress lacked the power: id. at 610–611.

The argument went too far: id at 611, 618; **legislative grace**: id at 615–616; **specter**: id at 616; **"truly national"**: id. at 599; **quotations of Marshall**: id. at 618 quoting *Cohens v. State of Virginia*, 19 U.S. 264, 426, and 428 (1821).

"It is State action...that is prohibited": *The Civil Rights Cases*, 109 U.S. 3, 11 (1883); invalidating the Civil Rights Act, of March 1, 1875, ch. 114, §§1–2, 18 St. 335. *The Civil Rights Cases* were the "judicial fulfillment of the Compromise of 1877" that permitted the election of Benjamin Harrison. See C. Vann Woodward, *Origins of the New South* (Baton Rouge: Louisiana State University Press, 1971) 216.

"intimate knowledge": *Morrison*, 529 U.S. 598 at 599.

Lynching was beyond federal law: *United States v. Harris*, 106 U.S. 629 (1883); U.S. Rev. Stat., ch. 7, §5519 (1873) (originally Act of April 20, 1871, ch. 22, §2, 17 St. 13, 14).

"'Careful adherence'": *Morrison*, 529 U.S. 598 at 622, quoting *Lugar v. Edmondson Oil Co.*, 457 U.S. 922, 936 (1982).

"a brutal assault": id. at 627; **"The omitted portions...shock and offend"**: id. at 601.

a "mountain of data": id. at 628–635 (Souter, J., dissenting, joined by Stevens, Ginsburg, and Breyer, JJ.); **"the most thorough legislative consideration"**: *Morrison*, 529 U.S. 598 at 631, quoting *Hodel v. Virginia Surface Min. and Reclamation Ass'n, Inc.*, 452 U.S. 264, 278–279 (1981); **"thousands to millions of dollars"**: id. at 635.

"The power...is complete in itself...": *Gibbons v. Ogden*, 22 U.S. 1, 196 (1824).

"a step toward recapturing": id. at 643; **"proper sphere"**: id. at 644; **"no general doctrine"**: *Maryland v. Wirtz*, 342 U.S. 183, 195 (1968), *Morrison* at 645; **"inviolable state spheres"**: id. at 646.

"single government": *Gibbons*, 22 U.S. 1 at 197.

Carter v. Carter Coal Co.: 298 U.S. 238 (1936).

Robert Jackson: *The Struggle for Judicial Supremacy* 160, quoted in *Morrison*, 529 U.S. 598 at 654 (Souter, J., dissenting).

"in the main": id. at 665; **"answer the §5 question":** id. at 666. Under some civil rights laws, state and institutional actors have been found liable if they engage in a "pattern or practice" of discrimination, or if they have a "custom" of encouraging violations of rights. Cf. *Bazenmore v. Friday*, 478 U.S. 223 (1988) (states liable under Title VII if a "pattern or practice" of discrimination is demonstrated); *Monell v. Dept. of Social Services*, 436 U.S. 658, 690 (imposing §1983 liability on municipalities for a specific event if a custom of encouraging such violations is demonstrated). Brzonkala's case against Virginia Tech was not significantly different. If in that case she had been given the opportunity to show a custom or practice of shielding athletes from the consequences of their violations of women's rights, the situation would be analogous to state action under Title VII.

duty and failure to act (torts): American Law Institute, *Restatement (Second) of Torts*, §284 (St. Paul, Minn.: American Law Institute Publishers, 1965); **duty and failure to act (trusts):** American Law Institute, *Restatement (Second) of Trusts*, §201 (St. Paul Minn.: American Law Institute Publishers, 1957). An even broader approach to congressional power is argued by Jack M. Balkin and Sanford Levinson, "Understanding the Constitutional Revolution," 87 *Va. L. Rev.* 1045, 1100 (2001).

special circumstances involving racial discrimination: *Reitman v. Mulkey*, 387 U.S. 369 (1967) (amendment to state constitution invalidating fair housing laws held to be state action violating equal protection); *Burton v. Wilmington Parking Authority*, 365 U.S. 715 (1961); see also Robert C. Post and Reva B. Siegel, "Equal Protection by Law," 110 *Yale L. J.*, 441, 503–05 (2001); Judith Resnik, "Categorical Federalism," *Yale L. J.*, 619 (2001).

CHAPTER 7

SOVEREIGN REMEDY

the "least dangerous" department: Alexander Hamilton, Number 78, *The Federalist.*

Intellectual Property Act proposed...in 1999: S. 1835 ("Intellectual Property Restoration Act of 1999"), 106th Cong., 1999, text introduced by Senator Leahy at 145 *Cong. Rec.* S13555–65 (1999).

Religious Liberty Protection Act: See H.R. Rep. 106–219 (1999).

secular saints: See G. Edward White, "The Canonization of Holmes and Brandeis: Epistemology and Judicial Reputations," 70 *N.Y.U. L. Rev.* 576 (1995).

The decision in *Bush v. Gore*: *Bush v. Gore*, 531 U.S. 98 (2000).

"neither Force nor Will": Alexander Hamilton, Number 78, *The Federalist.*

the waiver required by the Intellectual Property Act: See S. 1835 ("Intellectual Property Restoration Act of 1999") §111, 106th Cong., 1999, 145 *Cong. Rec.* at S13560 (1999).

condition federal funding: See *College Savings Bank v. Florida Prepaid Postsecondary Education Expense Board*, 527 U.S. 666, 686–687 (1999) (citing *South Dakota v. Dole*, 483 U.S. 203 (1987), which upheld Congress's use of spending power over highway funds to pressure states to raise drinking age to twenty-one); forced states to set speed limits: See 23 U.S.C. §141 (1994), repealed by National Highway System Designation Act of 1995 §204(d), 109 Stat. 568, 577 (1995). David Meltzer has made a careful study of action Congress could take to provide damages for infringement by states of federal patent, copyright, and trademark law. His conclusion is that "the most promising alternative, although hardly a sure-fire one," would be to condition federal funding of a state's programs on waiver of its immunity from suit on these subjects. See Meltzer,

"Overcoming Immunity: The Case of Federal Regulation of Intellectual Property," 53 *Stan. L. Rev.* 1331, 1389 (2001). As Meltzer observes, the easy extension of this approach to the other legislation where the Supreme Court has acknowledged state immunity makes it doubtful that the present majority would accept it. Id. at 1379.

combined two incongruous areas: Religious Land Use and Institutionalized Persons Act of 2000, Pub. L. 106–274, 114 Stat. 803 (September 22, 2000), codified at 42 U.S.C. §2000cc and elsewhere in 42 U.S.C.; **The Religious Liberty Protection Act:** See H.R. Rep. 106–219 at 12–13 (1999).

duty of lawyers to work to reform the law: American Bar Association, *Model Code of Professional Responsibility*, Canon 8 (1983); **judges' right to speak and write for the improvement of the law:** American Bar Association, *Code of Judicial Conduct*, Canon 4 (1990).

No defensible theory of the constitution justifies the justices...: See Akhil Reed Amar, "The Supreme Court 1999 Term. Foreword: The Document and the Doctrine," 114 *Harv. L. Rev.* 26, 83–84. State sovereign immunity has been attacked as "inconsistent with the supremacy of the Constitution and federal statutes, the basic principle of government accountability, and the central requirements of due process of law." See Erwin Chermerinsky, "Against Sovereign Immunity," 53 *Stan. L. Rev.* 1201, 1216 (2001).

the penalties of Purgatory: Dante Alighieri, *Commedia divina*, Canto 10 (the proud), Canto 13 (the envious), Canto 27 (the lustful).

The justices are all acting as legislators: see Amar, "The Supreme Court," 114 *Harv. L. Rev.* at 84, n.194, noting that under its present chief, the court has invalidated 24 acts of Congress, a number far outstripping the invalidations effected by any previous Supreme Court. The court under John Marshall, its chief from 1801 to 1832, held invalid a single congressional enactment.

that role being remedial: See *City of Richmond v. J. A. Croson Co.*, 488 U.S. 469, 487–488 (1989).

The preventative could be encompassed by the remedial: See *e.g.*, *Fullilove v. Klutznick*, 448 U.S. 448 (1980), overruled by *Adarand Constructors, Inc. v. Pena*, 515 U.S. 200 (1995) (constitutionality of federal affirmative action statute applied preventatively); *United Jewish Org. of Williamsburgh v. Carey*, 430 U.S. 144, 161 (1977) (rejecting proposition that racial criteria for redistricting can be used only as specific remedy for past unconstitutional apportionments.

The states appear in the original constitution: See U.S. constitution, art. I, sec. 2 (determining electors to House of Representatives and apportioning representatives by state); art. I, sec. 3 (states' role in apportionment and election of senators); art. II, sec. 1 (states' role in choosing electors); art. I, sec. 8 (reserving to the states the right to appoint officers to the militia and granting Congress power to purchase land from the states); art. I, sec. 9 (slave trade clause); art. III, sec. 2 (states as litigants); art. IV, sec. 1 (Full Faith and Credit clause); art. IV, sec. 2 (Privileges and Immunities clause); art. IV, sec. 2 (fugitive slave clause); art. IV, sec. 3 (states immune from division or merger); art. V (amending the constitution). **By amendment of the constitution:** U.S. constitution, amend. 10 (reserving nondelegated powers to the states or the people); U.S. constitution, amend. 11 (restricting judicial power of the United States); U.S. constitution, amend. 12 (procedures for electing president); U.S. constitution, amend. 17 (election of senators); U.S. constitution, amend. 21 (regulating importation of alcohol by states).

The states are expressly forbidden: U.S. constitution, art. I, sec. 10; **The president may call to service:** U.S. constitution, art II, sec. 2; **Supremacy Clause:** U.S. constitution, art. VI.

"It is revolting to have no better reason for a rule of law than that so it was laid down in the time of Henry IV.": O. W. Holmes Jr., "The Path of the Law," 10 *Harv. L. Rev.*, 469 (1897).

INDEX

Compositor: Michael Bass & Associates
Text: 10/15 Janson
Display: Janson
Printer and Binder: Maple-Vail Manufacturing Group